Prepared in cooperation with the Madison River Fisheries Technical Advisory Committee
Bureau of Land Management, Montana Department of Environmental Quality,
Montana Fish, Wildlife and Parks, PPL-Montana, U.S. Department of Agriculture
Forest Service – Gallatin National Forest, U.S. Fish and Wildlife Service

Lateral and Vertical Channel Movement and Potential for Bed-Material Movement on the Madison River Downstream from Earthquake Lake, Montana

Scientific Investigations Report 2012–5024

U.S. Department of the Interior
U.S. Geological Survey

Lateral and Vertical Channel Movement and Potential for Bed-Material Movement on the Madison River Downstream from Earthquake Lake, Montana

By Katherine J. Chase and Peter M. McCarthy

Prepared in cooperation with the Madison River Fisheries Technical Advisory Committee
Bureau of Land Management
Montana Department of Environmental Quality
Montana Fish, Wildlife and Parks
PPL-Montana
U.S. Department of Agriculture – Gallatin National Forest
U.S. Fish and Wildlife Service

Scientific Investigations Report 2012–5024

U.S. Department of the Interior
U.S. Geological Survey

U.S. Department of the Interior
KEN SALAZAR, Secretary

U.S. Geological Survey
Marcia K. McNutt, Director

U.S. Geological Survey, Reston, Virginia: 2012

For more information on the USGS—the Federal source for science about the Earth, its natural and living resources, natural hazards, and the environment, visit http://www.usgs.gov or call 1–888–ASK–USGS.

For an overview of USGS information products, including maps, imagery, and publications, visit http://www.usgs.gov/pubprod

To order this and other USGS information products, visit http://store.usgs.gov

Suggested citation:
Chase, K.J., and McCarthy, P.M., 2012, Lateral and vertical channel movement and potential for bed-material movement on the Madison River downstream from Earthquake Lake, Montana: U.S. Geological Survey Scientific Investigations Report 2012–5024, 39 p.

ISBN 978-1-4113-3363-5

Acknowledgments

The creative assistance of Kevin L. Sattler, Sean M. Lawlor (U.S. Geological Survey), and William G. Stotts (U.S. Geological Survey, retired) in surveying the deep and fast parts of the Madison River is gratefully acknowledged. Using various techniques such as diving and kayaking, they made every effort to survey as much of the channel as safely possible. Reviews by Stephen M. Wiele (U.S. Geological Survey) and John G. Elliott (U.S. Geological Survey, retired), are greatly appreciated.

The author also gratefully acknowledges Mark Story, Bruce Roberts, and Scott Barndt (U.S. Department of Agriculture Forest Service – Gallatin National Forest), and Brent Mabbot (PPL-Montana) for their assistance with reviews.

Contents

Figures

Tables

Conversion Factors, Datum, Acronyms, and Symbols

Inch/Pound to SI

Multiply	By	To obtain
cubic foot (ft³)	0.02832	cubic meter (m³)
cubic foot per second (ft³/s)	0.02832	cubic meter per second (m³/s)
inch (in.)	25.4	millimeter (mm)
foot (ft)	0.3048	meter (m)
foot per foot (ft/ft)	1.0	meter per meter (m/m)
gallon (gal)	3.785	liter (L)
mile (mi)	1.609	kilometer (km)
pound, avoirdupois (lb)	0.4536	kilogram (kg)
pound per square foot (lb/ft²)	0.04788	kilopascal (kPa)
pound per cubic foot (lb/ft³)	16.02	kilogram per cubic meter (kg/m³)
square mile (mi²)	2.590	square kilometer (km²)

Vertical coordinate information is referenced to the National Geodetic Vertical Datum of 1929 (NGVD 29).

Horizontal coordinate information is referenced to the North American Datum of 1983 (NAD 83).

Elevation, as used in this report, refers to distance above the vertical datum.

Water year, as used in this report, refers to the 12-month period October 1 through September 30. It is designated by the calendar year in which it ends.

Acronyms used in this report:

CD-ROM	Compact Disc–Read-Only Memory
EROS	U.S. Geological Survey Earth Resources Observation Systems
GNF	Gallatin National Forest
GPS	global positioning system
MADTAC	Madison River Fisheries Technical Advisory Committee
MDT	Montana Department of Transportation
NAD 83	North American Datum of 1983
NAIP	National Agriculture Imagery Program
NAPP	National Aerial Photography Program
NGVD 29	National Geodetic Datum of 1929
NHAP	National High Altitude Photography
NRIS	Montana Natural Resources Information System
RM	reference mark
RMSE	root-mean-square error
USDA	U.S. Department of Agriculture
USGS	U.S. Geological Survey
USACE	U.S. Army Corps of Engineers

Symbols and variables used in this report:

+/-	Plus or minus
D_x	Sediment size for which "x" percent of material is finer by weight or by number, in mm or ft
R	Hydraulic radius of the stream, or the cross-sectional area divided by the wetted perimeter, in ft
S	Energy slope, in ft/ft
γ	Specific weight of water (62.4 lb/ft^3)
γ_s	Specific weight of sediment, assumed to be 2.65 times the specific weight of water, in lb/ft^3
σ_g	Gradation coefficient, equal to the square root of the ratio D_{84}/D_{16}, dimensionless
τ_c	Critical shear stress, in lb/ft^2
$\tau(D_x)$	Critical shear stress for D_x, in lb/ft^2
τ^*_c	Dimensionless critical shear stress, or Shields parameter
τ_o	Mean boundary-shear stress, in lb/ft^2

Lateral and Vertical Channel Movement and Potential for Bed-Material Movement on the Madison River Downstream from Earthquake Lake, Montana

By Katherine J. Chase and Peter M. McCarthy

Abstract

The 1959 Hebgen Lake earthquake caused a massive landslide (Madison Slide) that dammed the Madison River and formed Earthquake Lake. The U.S. Army Corps of Engineers excavated a spillway through the Madison Slide to permit out-flow from Earthquake Lake. In June 1970, high streamflows on the Madison River severely eroded the spillway channel and damaged the roadway embankment along U.S. Highway 287 downstream from the Madison Slide. Investigations undertaken following the 1970 flood events concluded that substantial erosion through and downstream from the spillway could be expected for streamflows greater than 3,500 cubic feet per second (ft^3/s). Accordingly, the owners of Hebgen Dam, upstream from Earthquake Lake, have tried to man-age releases from Hebgen Lake to prevent streamflows from exceeding 3,500 ft^3/s measured at the U.S. Geological Survey (USGS) gaging station 0638800 Madison River at Kirby Ranch, near Cameron, Montana.

Management of flow releases from Hebgen Lake to avoid exceeding the threshold streamflow at USGS gaging station 06038800 is difficult, and has been questioned for two reasons. First, no road damage was reported downstream from the Earthquake Lake outlet in 1993, 1996, and 1997 when streamflows exceeded the 3,500-ft^3/s threshold. Second, the 3,500-ft^3/s threshold generally precludes releases of higher flows that could be beneficial to the blue-ribbon trout fishery downstream in the Madison River.

In response to concerns about minimizing streamflow downstream from Earthquake Lake and the possible armoring of the spillway, the USGS, in cooperation with the Madison River Fisheries Technical Advisory Committee (MADTAC; Bureau of Land Management; Montana Department of Environmental Quality; Montana Fish, Wildlife and Parks; PPL-Montana; U.S. Department of Agriculture Forest Ser-vice – Gallatin National Forest; and U.S. Fish and Wildlife Service), conducted a study to determine movement of the Madison River channel downstream from Earthquake Lake and to investigate the potential for bed material movement along the same reach. The purpose of this report is to present information about the lateral and vertical movement of the Madison River from 1970 to 2006 for a 1-mile reach down-stream from Earthquake Lake and for Raynolds Pass Bridge, and to provide an analysis of the potential for bed-material movement so that MADTAC can evaluate the applicability of the previously determined threshold streamflow for initiation of damaging erosion.

As part of this study channel cross sections originally surveyed by the USGS in 1971 were resurveyed in 2006. Incremental channel-movement distances were determined by comparing the stream centerlines from 14 aerial photographs taken between 1970 and 2006. Depths of channel incision and aggregation were determined by comparing the 2006 and 1971 cross-section and water-surface data. Particle sizes of bed and bank materials were measured in 2006 and 2008 using the pebble-count method and sieve analyses. A one-dimensional hydraulic-flow model (HEC-RAS) was used to calculate mean boundary-shear stresses for various streamflows; these cal-culated boundary-shear stresses were compared to calculated critical-shear stresses for the bed materials to determine the potential for bed-material movement.

A comparison of lateral channel movement distances with annual peak streamflows shows that streamflows higher than the 3,500-ft^3/s threshold were followed by lateral channel movement except from 1991 to 1992 and possibly from 1996 to 1997. However, it was not possible to discern whether the channel moved gradually or suddenly, or in response to one peak flow, to several peak flows, or to sustained flows. The channel moved between 2002 and 2005 even when stream-flows were less than the threshold streamflow of 3,500 ft^3/s.

Comparisons of cross sections and aerial photographs show that the channel has moved laterally and incised and aggraded to varying degrees. The channel has developed meander bends and has incised as much as 5–12 feet (ft) through the upstream part of the Madison Slide (cross sections 1400–800). Near cross section 800, the stream has eroded into the steep right bank between the stream and the road where fill was mechanically placed after 1970. Channel movement also was noted downstream from the Madison Slide.

Near Raynolds Pass Bridge, about 3 miles (mi) down-stream from Earthquake Lake, elevations across the channel have changed by -1.4 ft to +1.9 ft, but these changes were local in nature and could represent a few rocks or depressions in the bed. Overall, it does not appear that the materials eroded from the Madison Slide are causing aggradation in the subreach near the Raynolds Pass Bridge.

Comparisons of critical shear stresses to mean boundary-shear stresses indicate that the D_{50} particle sizes (median size) along the right side of the bed between cross sections 400 and 500 and along the right side of the bed between cross sections 1300 and 1400 could move at the threshold streamflow. In contrast, most of the D_{84} particle sizes at those two locations probably will not move at the threshold streamflow. This lack of movement for the larger particles at the threshold streamflow could lead to further armoring of the bed as the D_{50} and smaller-sized particles are removed from the bed and transported downstream.

The Shields parameter values from 0.04 to 0.08 that were used to calculate critical shear stresses could be conservative for a high-gradient stream such as the Madison. A higher, less conservative, Shields parameter would result in higher critical shear stresses, meaning that higher streamflows would be required to move material than those reported herein. In addition, because materials in the channel thalweg are exposed to higher boundary-shear stresses than the materials along the sides of the channel, larger, more erosion-resistant materials likely exist in the deeper parts of the channel where high-flow depths and velocities prevented sediment sampling. Movement of these materials might require higher critical shear stresses than estimated in this report. Characterization of sediment sizes in the center of the stream and observation of bed-material movement for a range of streamflows could provide information to help refine the Shields parameter and critical-shear stress estimates for bed materials in the Madison River downstream from Earthquake Lake. Furthermore, resurveying cross sections and water-surface elevations more frequently (either annually or after high streamflows) could better define the relation between streamflow and lateral and vertical channel movement.

Introduction

On August 17, 1959, a severe earthquake, centered near the Madison River north of Hebgen Lake, caused a massive landslide (Madison Slide; Hadley, 1964). The Madison Slide created an earthen dam that impeded the flow of the Madison River and formed Earthquake Lake (locally referred to as Quake Lake, fig. 1). The U.S. Army Corps of Engineers (USACE) constructed a relatively straight spillway through the Madison Slide to permit outflow from Earthquake Lake. The Madison River channel through the Madison Slide downstream from Earthquake Lake typically is referred to as the "spillway;" the channel just downstream from Earthquake Lake is referred to as the "Earthquake Lake outlet." Since 1959, the channel sinuosity has increased through the spillway. Downstream from the Madison Slide (downstream from cross

section 700, fig. 2), the channel has migrated both to the right and to the left across the valley.

In June 1970, high streamflows in the Madison River severely eroded the spillway and damaged the roadway embankment along U.S. Highway 287 north of the channel (fig. 1). Flooding in 1971 and 1986 caused additional erosion of the spillway channel and roadway embankment. As a result of the flooding and erosional damage in 1970 and 1971, several studies were undertaken to assess the stability of the Madison Slide area and to mitigate future erosional flood damage. Based on these studies, the USACE determined that streamflows greater than 3,500 cubic feet per second (ft^3/s) could result in substantial erosion through and downstream from the spillway (U.S. Army Corps of Engineers, 1972). Therefore, PPL-Montana, the current (2011) owner of Hebgen Dam upstream from Earthquake Lake, has tried to manage releases from Hebgen Lake to prevent streamflows [as measured at U.S. Geological Survey (USGS) streamflow-gaging station (gaging station) 06038800] from exceeding 3,500 ft^3/s.

Management of flow releases from Hebgen Lake to prevent streamflows at USGS gaging station 06038800 from exceeding the 3,500-ft^3/s threshold streamflow is difficult. Flooding of Cabin Creek and Beaver Creek, which enter the Madison River between Hebgen Lake and the Earthquake Lake outlet, can cause streamflows at the outlet and at gaging station 06038800 to exceed the 3,500-ft^3/s threshold streamflow even when streamflow releases from Hebgen Lake are minimal.

The 3,500-ft^3/s threshold streamflow has been questioned for two main reasons. First, no road damage was reported downstream from the Earthquake Lake outlet in 1993, 1996, and 1997 when streamflows exceeded the 3,500-ft^3/s threshold. This lack of road damage during relatively high streamflows might indicate that the channel has become armored and is no longer as susceptible to erosion as it was in the 1970s and 1980s. Secondly, the 3,500-ft^3/s threshold generally precludes releases of higher flows that could be beneficial to the blue-ribbon trout fishery downstream in the Madison River (Montana Fish, Wildlife and Parks, 2010).

In response to the concerns about minimizing streamflows downstream from Earthquake Lake and about the possible armoring of the spillway, the USGS, in cooperation with the Madison River Fisheries Technical Advisory Committee (MADTAC; Bureau of Land Management; Montana Department of Environmental Quality; Montana Fish, Wildlife and Parks; PPL-Montana;, U.S. Department of Agriculture Forest Service – Gallatin National Forest; and U.S. Fish and Wildlife Service), conducted a study to determine the lateral and vertical channel movement from 1970 to 2006 for an approximately 1-mi reach of the Madison River downstream from Earthquake Lake. Channel changes at the bridge on State Highway 87 (Raynolds Pass Bridge) also were assessed. Furthermore, the potential for moving bed material at various streamflows was estimated in order to help MADTAC determine whether the threshold streamflow of 3,500 ft^3/s was still applicable for the initiation of damaging erosion.

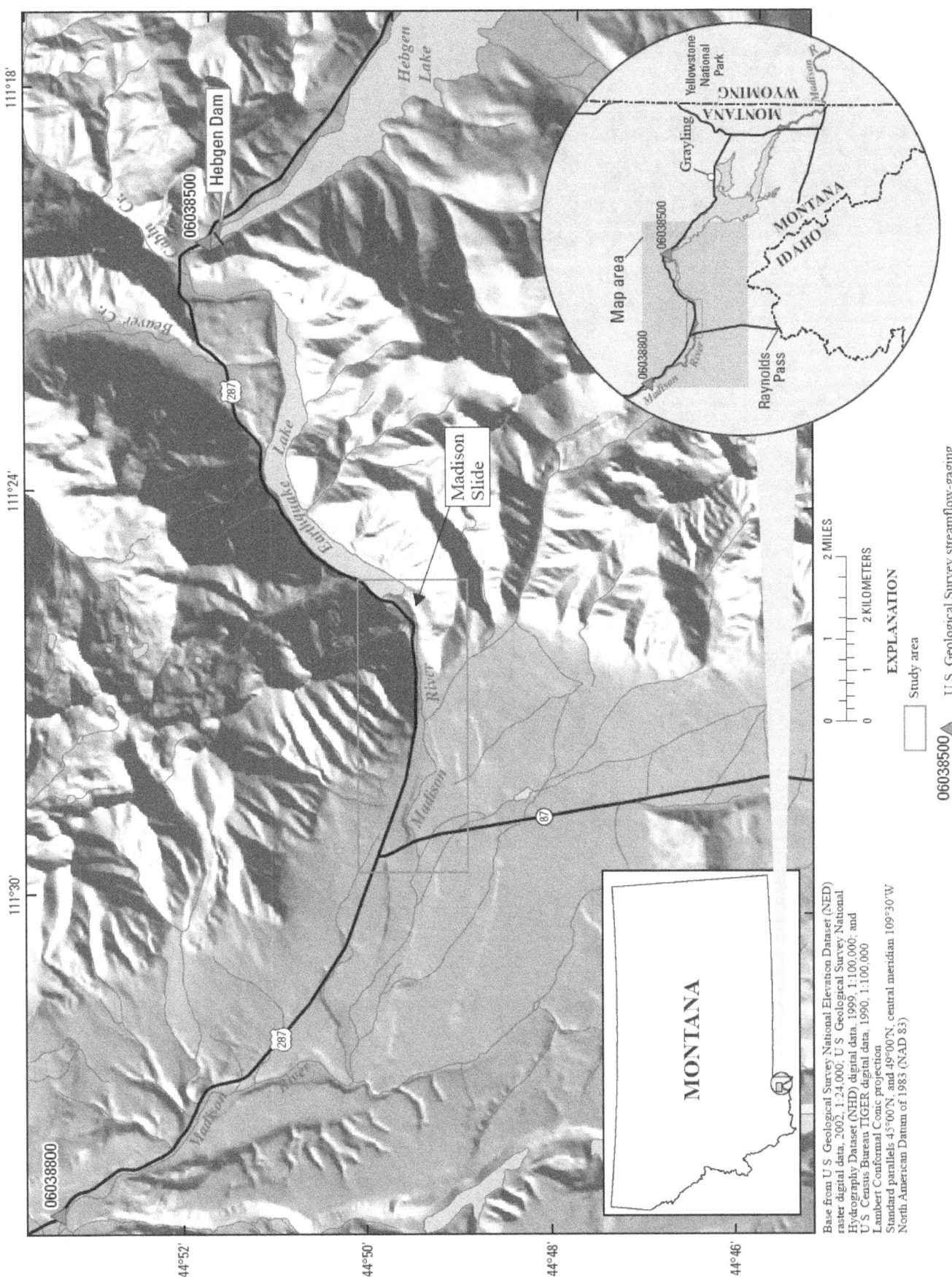

Figure 1. Location of study area.

Base from U S Geological Survey National Elevation Dataset (NED)
raster digital data, 2002, 1:24,000; U S Geological Survey National
Hydrography Dataset (NHD) digital data, 1999, 1:100,000; and
U S Census Bureau TIGER digital data, 1990, 1:100,000
Lambert Conformal Conic projection
Standard parallels 45°00'N and 49°00'N, central meridian 109°30'W
North American Datum of 1983 (NAD 83)

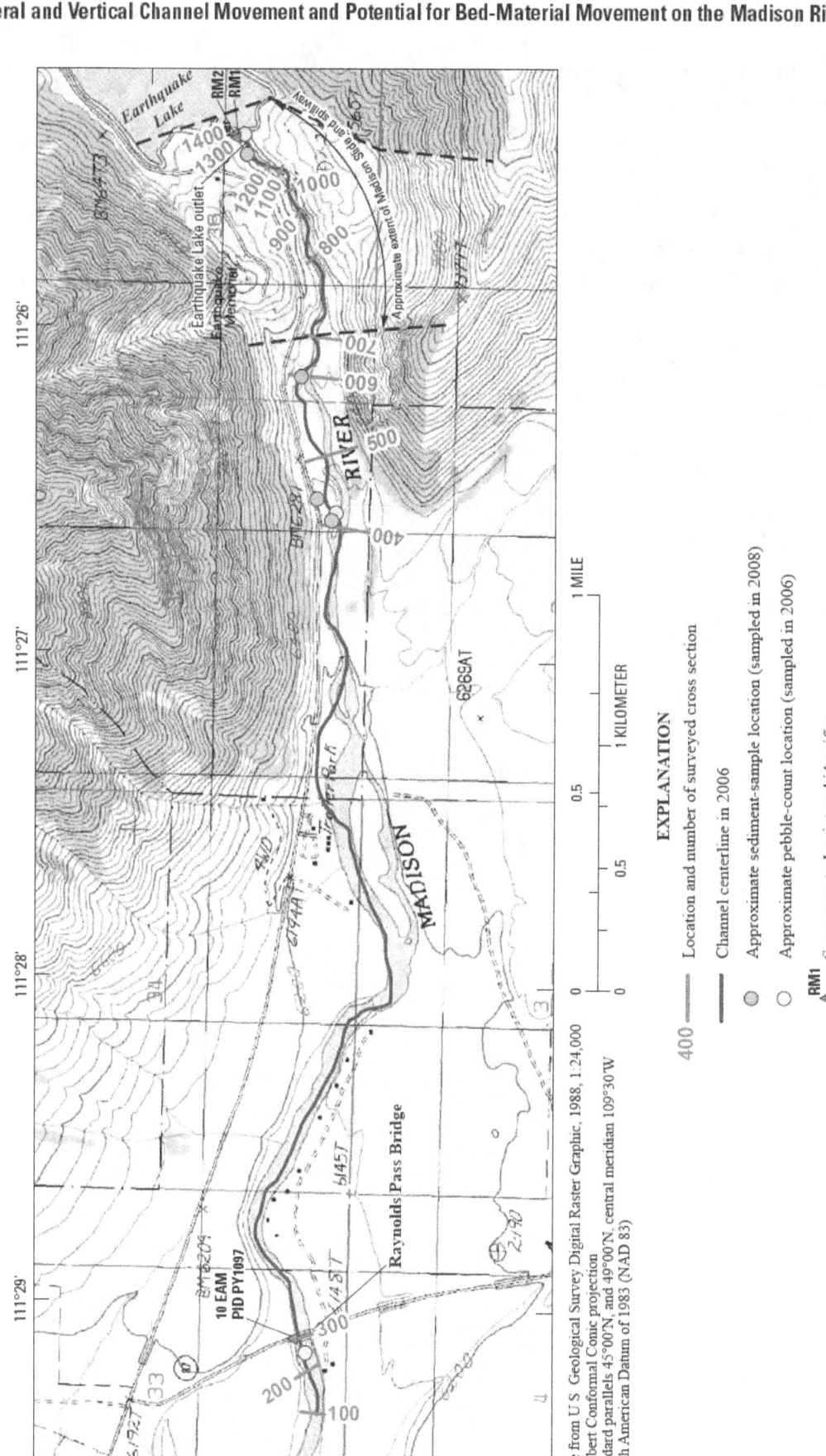

Base from U S Geological Survey Digital Raster Graphic, 1988, 1:24,000
Lambert Conformal Conic projection
Standard parallels 45°00'N, and 49°00'N, central meridian 109°30'W
North American Datum of 1983 (NAD 83)

EXPLANATION

400 ——— Location and number of surveyed cross section

——— Channel centerline in 2006

● Approximate sediment-sample location (sampled in 2008)

○ Approximate pebble-count location (sampled in 2006)

▲ RM1 Survey control point and identifier

Figure 2. Location of surveyed cross sections, channel centerline in 2006, approximate locations of sediment samples collected in 2006 and 2008, and survey reference marks along the Madison River downstream from Earthquake Lake, Montana.

Purpose and Scope

The purpose of this report is to present information about the lateral and vertical movement of the Madison River from 1970 to 2006 for a 1-mi reach downstream from Earthquake Lake and for Raynolds Pass Bridge, and to provide an analysis of the potential for bed-material movement so that MADTAC can evaluate the applicability of the 3,500-ft^3/s threshold streamflow for initiation of damaging erosion. Survey data from 1960, 1971, 1975 and 2006 and aerial photographs from 1970 through 2006 were used to quantify lateral and vertical channel movement. Particle-size data and hydraulic analyses were used to estimate the potential for bed-material movement at various streamflows. Supplemental particle-size data were collected in 2008.

Also, the report provides one Compact Disc–Read-Only Memory (CD–ROM) that includes appendix 1 at the back of this report on the inside back cover. This appendix contains aerial photographs (figs. A–1 through A–9) with the locations of cross sections and centerlines for the Madison River.

Description of the Study Area

The Madison River flows westerly from Yellowstone National Park into Hebgen Lake, where flow releases are controlled by a dam built in 1915. The Madison Slide is located about 6 miles (mi) downstream from Hebgen Lake (fig. 1). Earthquake Lake is approximately 4 mi long; its inlet is located about 2 mi downstream from Hebgen Lake. Between Hebgen Dam and Earthquake Lake, Cabin Creek flows into the Madison River from the north. Beaver Creek flows into Earthquake Lake from the north. The Madison River flows westerly 3 mi from Earthquake Lake and then flows northerly.

Currently (2011) there is no gaging station at the Earthquake Lake outlet. The USGS operates two gaging stations on the Madison River near Earthquake Lake (fig. 1): Madison River below Hebgen Lake, near Grayling, Mont., (06038500) upstream from Earthquake Lake ["upstream gage," drainage area 905 square miles (mi^2)], and Madison River at Kirby Ranch, near Cameron, Mont., (06038800) downstream from Earthquake Lake ("downstream gage," drainage area 1,065 mi^2). The 3,500-ft^3/s threshold streamflow is referenced to the downstream gage. The drainage area between the upstream gage and the Earthquake Lake outlet is about 90 mi^2 (U.S. Army Corps of Engineers, 1972). Therefore the drainage area at the Earthquake Lake outlet is about 995 mi^2, and is closer to the drainage area at the downstream gage than the drainage area at the upstream gage. Thus the streamflows at the downstream gage are assumed to be equal to the streamflows through the Madison Slide downstream from Earthquake Lake for this study. On the basis of the flood-frequency information for the downstream gage, the 3,500-ft^3/s threshold streamflow occurs about every 2 to 5 years within the study reach (table 1).

Table 1.   Recurrence intervals and corresponding annual peak streamflow data for two gaging stations near the study area[1].

[Upstream gage, U.S. Geological Survey (USGS) streamflow-gaging station 06038500, Madison River below Hebgen Lake, near Grayling, Mont.; downstream gage, USGS streamflow-gaging station 06038800, Madison River at Kirby Ranch, near Cameron, Mont. Abbreviation: ft^3/s, cubic feet per second]

Recurrence interval (years)	Annual peak streamflow upstream gage (ft^3/s)	Annual peak streamflow downstream gage (ft^3/s)
2	2,510	2,910
5	3,160	4,270
10	3,600	5,180
25	4,160	6,320

[1]From Parrett and Johnson (2004).

Previous Investigations

In May and September of 1971, Johnson and Omang (1972) surveyed water-surface profiles and 14 cross sections along the Madison River downstream from Earthquake Lake. They compared these profiles with water-surface profiles surveyed by the USACE in 1960 and determined that the channel through the Madison Slide had incised by up to 19 feet (ft). Johnson and Omang (1972) further concluded that channel through the spillway had incised by about 8 ft during the spring and summer runoff events in 1971.

The USACE conducted hydraulic studies to determine the maximum streamflow that could be discharged downstream from Earthquake Lake without substantially eroding the spillway or damaging the highway downstream from the slide (U.S. Army Corps of Engineers, 1972). The USACE report included sediment-size data for the bed and streambanks downstream from Earthquake Lake and analyses of velocities and streamflows necessary for bed-material movement. The USACE estimated that flows of about 3,500 ft^3/s could erode the steeper parts of the spillway and produce downstream deposition, initiate channel movement and bank erosion, and potentially damage highway embankments.

Methods

Surveys of the Madison River Channel

Data from the 1971 survey (Johnson and Omang, 1972) were used to determine the approximate locations of the cross sections surveyed for this study. For the 1971 survey, each of the 14 cross sections was referenced to a hub. Though northing and easting coordinates for each hub could be calculated from data in the survey notes, only distance and elevation data were available for the surveyed points along each cross section. Locations of the cross sections were estimated using the hub locations, 1970 and 1976 aerial photographs, and sketches from the project files. Of the 14 cross sections, 11 were within about 1 mi of the Earthquake Lake outlet, and the other 3 were approximately 3.5 mi downstream from the outlet near Raynolds Pass Bridge (fig. 2).

Cross sections were resurveyed as closely as possible to the locations of the 1971 cross sections given that the channel changed between 1971 and 2006, and the exact coordinates and alignment of the 1971 cross sections were unknown. Survey-grade global positioning system (GPS) equipment and a total station were used to resurvey location and elevation data along the 14 cross sections (fig. 2). Cross sections were numbered from downstream to upstream. Cross sections 100, 200, and 300 are near Raynolds Pass Bridge (fig. 2). Cross sections 400, 500, and 600 are downstream from the Madison Slide, cross section 700 is near the downstream boundary of the Madison Slide (end of the spillway), and cross section 1400 is at the Earthquake Lake outlet.

Water-surface elevations were surveyed in 2006 along the channel from Earthquake Lake outlet to Raynolds Pass Bridge. The 2006 water-surface profiles were compared to 1960 and 1971 water-surface profiles published in Johnson and Omang (1972). In addition, survey notes and drawings containing a water-surface profile from 1975 were compiled for this study. However, because of turbulence and waves, the water-surface elevations through the study reach were difficult to survey. During the surveys the water-surface elevations at a single location on the Madison River were observed to change by at least 0.3 ft several times per minute.

Cross sections and channel features are described using a USGS convention in which features are referenced in a down-stream view from left to right. For example, the right bank was considered to be on the right-hand side of an observer when looking downstream.

Flows through most of the study reach were too deep and fast to wade. In 1971 and in 2006, survey personnel waded as far into the stream as was safe and then estimated the remaining depths of the cross section. In 2006, the survey personnel observed that these estimated thalweg elevations probably were within -5 to +2 ft of actual thalweg elevations. Only cross sections 100, 200, 300 (near the Raynolds Pass Bridge) and 1400 (the most upstream cross section) were entirely wadeable.

The elevations and horizontal coordinates for the 2006 survey were calculated from three reference marks (RMs) along the Madison River used for the 1971 survey. One RM is a National Geodetic Survey control point (designation 10 EAM, PID PY1097) near the Raynolds Pass Bridge. The USGS established the other two RMs in 1971: steel posts on the right bank of the Madison River just downstream from Earthquake Lake (RM 1 and RM 2, fig. 2). A report by Foundation and Materials Consultants, Inc. (1972) states that between 1959 and 1972 the Madison Slide settled 5 ft. After 1972, settlement could have affected the elevations of the two USGS RMs. However, from examination of the settlement curve (Foundation and Materials Consultants, Inc., 1972), it appears that minimal (less than 1.5 ft) settlement could be

expected to occur between 1972 and 2006. Given that no other reference elevations or data were available to determine post-1972 settlement, the USGS RM elevations established in 1972 were used for this study. For consistency with the 1971 survey and other published data, the 2006 survey was referenced to the National Geodetic Vertical Datum of 1929 (NGVD 29).

HEC-RAS Analysis

HEC-RAS version 4.0, a one dimensional, hydraulic-flow model developed by the U.S. Army Corps of Engineers (2008a, b, c), was used to calculate water-surface elevations and other hydraulic variables such as cross-sectional width, depth, and area, hydraulic radius, energy slope, and mean boundary-shear stress at surveyed cross sections 400 through 1400 for streamflows that ranged from 400 to 6,000 ft³/s. HEC-RAS inputs include streamflow, cross-section geometry, distances between cross sections, and Manning's roughness coefficients (Henderson, 1966). First, Manning's roughness coefficients (Henderson, 1966) were estimated for each cross section based on channel geometry, vegetation, and bed and bank particle sizes observed in the field and in photographs. Then, these coefficients were incrementally modified until calculated water-surface elevations were reasonably close to surveyed water-surface elevations for the streamflow at the time of the survey (1,040 ft³/s; http://waterdata.usgs.gov/mt/nwis). The resulting Manning's roughness coefficients ranged from 0.055 to 0.110. These relatively high values were considered reasonable due to the large boulders in many locations through the study reach. Calculated flow depths at the thalweg for the streamflow at the time of the survey (1,040 ft³/s) ranged from 3 to 8 ft. Differences between calculated and observed water-surface elevations were less than 0.9 ft at all cross sections and equal to or less than 0.5 ft at 8 of the 11 cross sections. Given the difficulty in surveying the fluctuating water surfaces, these differences can be considered reasonable. The similarity of the water-surface elevations calculated by HEC-RAS to the water-surface elevations that were surveyed indicates that the calculation errors attributed to the estimated thalweg elevations for the unwadeable portions of the cross sections did not substantially affect the study results.

Sediment Sampling

Sediment-size characteristics were determined for surficial bed material, large alluvial bars adjacent to low-flow channels, and streambanks by the pebble-count method (Wolman, 1954). Sediment-size distributions of the material below the bed and bank surfaces were determined by collecting sediment samples in 5-gallon buckets and conducting sieve analysis of the samples. The D_{50} (the median size, or particle size for which 50 percent of the sample material is finer) was determined by weight from the sieve analyses and by number of particles from the pebble counts. The D_{16}, D_{65}, and D_{84} (particle sizes for which 16, 65, and 84 percent of the sample materials are finer, respectively) were determined in the same manner.

Approximate sample locations are shown on figure 2. The pebble counts between cross sections 1300 and 1400 and between cross sections 400 and 500 were restricted by high flow depths and stream velocities to the right portions of the bed; these sampled portions extended approximately 25 percent of the distance across the channel. The pebble count between cross sections 100 and 300 was restricted to the left and right portions of the bed; the sampled portions of these sections extended into the channel approximately 25 percent of the distance across the channel. No pebble counts were conducted along the bed between cross sections 1200 and 600 due to high flow depths and stream velocities.

Aerial Photography Analysis

Aerial photographs taken between 1970 and 2006 were obtained from several sources (table 2). Aerial photographs from the years 1976, 1981, 1984, and 1986 were not available digitally; thus these photographs were scanned. The 1970–2005 photographs were transformed and rectified to match a common projection and datum. The 2006 digital orthophotograph was used as the reference to which the earlier photographs were rectified.

Incremental channel-movement distances were determined from a time series of the 14 aerial photographs taken between 1970 and 2006 (table 2, appendix 1). On each aerial photograph, two stream centerlines were drawn; one centerline corresponded to the stream location shown on the photograph for that current time period, and the other centerline corresponded to the stream location from the previous time period. In the more braided subreaches downstream from the Madison Slide, centerlines were drawn along the dominant flow-conveying channel at the date and streamflow corresponding to the aerial photograph. At higher streamflows, more than one of the braided channels could be inundated, and the differences between the centerlines would not be as dramatic. For example, the channel centerline in 1986, shown on figure A–4, was drawn along the stream channel closer to the road because that channel appeared larger and was judged to be the dominant flow-conveying channel. However at higher flows much of the streamflow also could have been flowing through one or more of the multiple channels south of that dominant flow-conveying channel. The distance between one of those multiple channels and the channel centerline in 1984 could be shorter than the distance between the channel centerlines shown on figure A–4 (depending on which of those multiple channels was chosen for measurement).

To assess the potential error in measuring distances between points on aerial photos from different years, test points were established at features visible on the aerial photographs. Seven or more test points could be located on 11 of the 14 aerial photographs. Fewer control points were visible on the other three aerial photographs because they did not include the entire study area and because some of the structures used as test points had not yet been built. The root-mean-square error (RMSE) was calculated for the easting (X) and the northing (Y) for the collection of test points on each transformed aerial photograph by using the equations:

$$RMSE(X_t) = \sqrt{(\sum_{1}^{n}(X_t - X_r)^2)/n}, \text{ and} \qquad (1)$$

$$RMSE(Y_t) = \sqrt{(\sum_{1}^{n}(Y_t - Y_r)^2)/n} \qquad (2)$$

where

$RMSE$	is the root-mean-square-error;
X_t	is the easting coordinate for the test point on the transformed image, in feet;
n	is the number of control points;
X_r	is the easting coordinate for the test point on the reference image, in feet;
Y_t	is the northing coordinate for the test point on the transformed image, in feet; and
Y_r	is the northing coordinate for the test point on the reference image, in feet.

RMSEs for the test points ranged from 0.40 to 14 ft (table 2). A stationary object on two aerial photographs associated with smaller RMSEs would have about the same coordinates, but the stationary object might appear to "move" between aerial photographs associated with larger RMSEs. To account for the potential error in measuring distances between channel centerlines from the aerial photographs, lateral distances are reported with an accuracy of plus or minus (+/-) 30 ft. At the narrowest subreach through cross section 1000, this potential +/- 30 ft error is almost equal to the width of the channel; in other subreaches the error is about 5–30 percent of channel width. If the distance measured between centerlines at a certain location along the river was less than 30 ft, channel movement was reported as zero at that location.

Aerial photographs from the years 1970, 1976, 1984, 1986, 1992, 1995, 2000, 2005, and 2006 are included in appendix 1 (figs. A–1 through A–9). Aerial photographs from the years 1980, 1981, 1987, 1990, and 2002 are not included in appendix 1 because substantial channel movement was not observed from those photographs, except for the 40 ft (+/- 30 ft) of movement at cross section 700 and movement towards the road about 0.25 mi downstream from cross section 400, both observed in the 1987 photograph.

Table 2.   Statistics from the digital processing and rectification of aerial photographs to the 2006 aerial photograph, Madison River below Earthquake Lake, Montana.

[Root-mean-square error, deviation between control-point coordinates on each rectified photograph and the control-point coordinates on the 2006 aerial photograph, calculated for the easting (X) and northing (Y) directions. Abbreviations: ft³/s, cubic feet per sencond; MDT, Montana Department of Transportation; GNF, Gallatin National Forest; EROS, U.S. Geological Survey Earth Resources Observation Systems; NHAP, National High Altitude Photography; NRIS, Montana Natural Resources Information System; NAIP, National Agriculture Imagery Program; NAPP, National Aerial Photography Program; USDA, U.S. Department of Agriculture; USGS, U.S. Geological Survey]

Photgraphy date	Source	Format	Number of control points	Root-mean-square error, easting (feet)	Root-mean-square error, northing (feet)	Daily mean streamflow on date of photograph (ft³/s)
6/19/1970	MDT[1]	Digital	1	0.40	2.5	[2]2,820
6/9/1976	GNF[3]	Paper copy	7	1.3	1.5	[2]1,040
9/4/1980	EROS NHAP[4]	Digital	8	1.2	2.6	[2]719
7/20/1981	GNF[3]	Paper copy	8	5.8	3.1	[5]999
7/31/1984	GNF[3]	Paper copy	3	2.4	4.6	[5]1,680
6/12/1986	GNF[3]	Paper copy	6	14	9.9	[5]3,400
9/6/1987	EROS NAPP[6]	Digital	10	11	8.0	[2]1,010
9/10/1990	EROS NAPP[6]	Digital	10	9.6	6.6	[5]995
7/29/1992	EROS NAPP[6]	Digital	10	11	7.5	[5]1,010
8/12/1995	EROS NAPP[6]	Digital	10	2.5	2.6	[2]1,100
9/7/2000	EROS NAPP[6]	Digital	10	13	8.6	[5]1,080
9/10/2002	EROS NAPP[6]	Digital	10	13	9.3	[5]968
8/20/2005	NRIS[7]	Digital	10	2.8	5.3	[5]1,110
July or August 2006	USDA NAIP[8]	Digital	10	0	0	[9]1,030–1,690

[1] Steve Barton, Montana Department of Transportation, written commun., 2008.

[2] Streamflow at USGS streamflow-gaging station Madison River below Hebgen Lake, near Grayling, Montana (06038500; *http //waterdata.usgs.gov/mt/nwis*).

[3] Jackie Riley, Gallatin National Forest, written commun., 2007.

[4] U.S. Geological Survey, 2007b.

[5] Streamflow at USGS streamflow-gaging station Madison River at Kirby Ranch, near Cameron, Montana (06038800; *http //waterdata.usgs.gov/mt/nwis*).

[6] U.S. Geological Survey, 2007a.

[7] Montana State Library, 2007.

[8] Laurie Temple, U.S. Geological Survey, written commun., 2008.

[9] Range of streamflows at USGS streamflow-gaging station Madison River at Kirby Ranch, near Cameron, Montana (06038800) for July 1, 2006, to August 31, 2006 (*http //waterdata.usgs.gov/mt/nwis*).

Lateral and Vertical Channel Movement

The Madison River has moved both laterally (lateral migration) and vertically (incision and aggradation) since the Madison Slide occurred in 1959. The Madison River through the spillway has steep longitudinal slopes [up to 0.046 feet per feet (ft/ft)] and, therefore, can transport large quantities of material from the bed and banks. Because Earthquake Lake tends to trap sediment, the spillway is prone to incision and lateral migration. Additionally, the channel banks along the spillway are extremely high (about 40 ft high in places; fig. 3) and bank slopes are almost equal to the angle of repose for the bank material. As the river undercuts the bank, large

amounts of material are deposited into the channel, further contributing to channel instability. In contrast, the longitudinal slopes downstream from the spillway are not as steep (about 0.014 ft/ft). Consequently, much of the material removed from the spillway can be deposited downstream, which can lead to channel aggradation, widening, and braiding downstream from the Madison Slide.

In this section, lateral movement measured from the time-series of aerial photographs is discussed. A positive value indicates lateral movement toward the right bank, and a negative value indicates lateral movement toward the left bank. Then, vertical movement measured and estimated from the channel surveys is discussed. Finally, a synopsis of lateral and vertical movement on a reach-by-reach basis is presented.

Figure 3. Madison River downstream from Earthquake Lake, Montana, looking downstream from right bank at cross section 1100.

Lateral Movement

Lateral movement (migration) of the Madison River channel near the Madison Slide was observed when embankments along U.S. Highway 287 were eroded in 1970. In the aerial photograph taken after the highway embankments were eroded (fig. A–1), U.S. Highway 287 is washed out from about 0.05 mi downstream from cross section 600 to about 0.25 mi downstream from cross section 400. Also in figure A–1, a steep cutbank is apparent above the right bank, just south of the road near cross section 800, indicating that the road near cross section 800 almost washed out as well.

Between 1970 and 1976, the aerial photographs show channel migration as well as fill placed along the channel. Figure A–2 shows that fill was mechanically placed at the steep cutbank on the right bank above cross section 800, and the channel shifted to the left away from the road. Fill also was placed between the channel and the road near cross section 600. Meanders of the main channel near cross sections 700 and 600 appear to have increased in amplitude and moved upstream about 100 ft. The channel generally migrated to the left away from the road from cross section 500 downstream to cross section 400 (fig. A–2, table 3). A new meander in the main channel formed about one-half mile downstream from cross section 400 towards the road.

Lateral migration between 1976 and 1986 is shown on figures A–3 and A–4. Between 1976 and 1984, the distances measured between the centerlines on the aerial photographs (fig. A–3) that were less than the potential rectification error (+/-30 ft) are reported as zero in table 3. Between 1984 and 1986 the river eroded the right bank at cross section 1200 and into the left bank at cross section 1100, forming new meander bends (fig. A–4, table 3). Comparison of photographs of the stream channel upstream from cross section 1100 shows this movement to the left (fig. 4). Because the left bank at cross section 1100 is high and steep (figs. 3 and 4), large amounts of sand, gravel, cobbles, and boulders probably entered the channel and were deposited downstream. Also between 1984 and 1986, the river eroded into the mechanically placed fill on the right bank near cross section 800 (figs. A–4, fig. 5, table 3).

Between 1984 and 1986, channel movement was more substantial downstream from the spillway (fig. A–4, table 3). The channel shifted toward the right bank (toward the road) downstream from cross section 600. The dead trees in the channel downstream from cross section 600 (fig. 6) likely grew prior to this 1984–1986 time period, before the channel shifted towards the right bank. The channel moved about 370 ft (+/- 30 ft) into the right bank between cross sections 500 and 400 (table 3), damaging the road.

Lateral migration distances between 1986 and 1992, measured between the centerlines in the aerial photographs (fig. A–5) were often less than the potential rectification error (+/-30 ft) and are reported as zero (table 3). The river generally eroded farther into the right bank downstream from cross section 800 (fig. A–5), but this movement occurred between cross sections 800 and 700 (not reported in table 3).

In the 13 years between 1992 and 2005, the Madison River channel continued to display considerable mobility. First, between 1992 and 1995, the channel shifted into the left bank at cross sections 1100, 900, 500, and 400 (fig. A–6, table 3). About 0.5 mi downstream from cross section 400, the channel moved approximately 530 ft (+/- 30 ft) into the right bank, closer to the road (fig. A–6). Then, between 1995 and 2000, the river moved into the left bank at cross section 400, and moved back to the right (towards the road) downstream from cross section 400 (table 3, fig. A–7). Between 2000 and 2005, the channel shifted into the left bank through much of the spillway (table 3; fig. A–8). Erosion into the left bank upstream from cross section 800 can be seen from the differences in the 1971 and 2006 photographs (fig. 7). Last, between 2005 and 2006, no changes were determined from the centerlines in the aerial photographs (table 3).

Centerlines of the Madison River from all of the aerial photographs (A–1 through A–8) are shown on the 2006 aerial photograph in figure A–9. The maximum lateral migration distances of the channel since 1970 (the maximum distances between the centerlines from all of the aerial photographs) were 560 ft at the downstream end of the study reach, 370 ft downstream from the spillway between cross sections 400 and 500, and 150 ft near the upstream end of the spillway near cross section 1100 (all distances are +/- 30 ft). This maximum lateral migration is less than the sum of incremental lateral migration measured from the aerial photographs because the channel did not migrate continuously in one direction throughout this period (1970–2006).

Table 3. Lateral channel movement and annual peak streamflows[1] for the Madison River, Montana.

[Negative value (-) indicates movement to the left bank (south), positive value indicates movement to the right bank (north). Abbreviations: +/-, plus or minus; ft, feet; USGS, U.S. Geological Survey; ft³/s, cubic feet per second. Symbol: -- data not available or not applicable]

Water year	Date of photography	Channel movement (+/-30 feet) at or between indicated cross sections, between indicated date and date of previous aerial photograph (ft)													Annual peak streamflow at USGS streamflow-gaging station			
		Earthquake Lake outlet	Spillway							Downstream from spillway					Madison River below Hebgen Lake, near Grayling, Mont. (06038500)		Madison River at Kirby Ranch, near Cameron, Mont. (06038800)	
		Cross section 1400	Cross section 1300	Cross section 1200	Cross section 1100	Cross section 1000	Cross section 900	Cross section 800	Cross section 700	Cross section 600	Between cross sections 600 and 500	Cross section 500	Between cross sections 500 and 400	Cross section 400	Date of streamflow	Streamflow (ft³/s)	Date of streamflow	Streamflow (ft³/s)
1959	--	--	--	--	--	--	--	--	--	--	--	--	--	--	8/17/1959	10,200	10/23/1959	4,710
1960	--	--	--	--	--	--	--	--	--	--	--	--	--	--	--	--	--	--
1961	--	--	--	--	--	--	--	--	--	--	--	--	--	--	7/5/1961	1,560	9/11/1961	1,470
1962	--	--	--	--	--	--	--	--	--	--	--	--	--	--	11/22/1961	2,660	--	--
1963	--	--	--	--	--	--	--	--	--	--	--	--	--	--	6/6/1963	2,510	6/5/1963	3,480
1964	--	--	--	--	--	--	--	--	--	--	--	--	--	--	6/19/1964	2,750	--	--
1965	--	--	--	--	--	--	--	--	--	--	--	--	--	--	6/29/1965	2,700	--	--
1966	--	--	--	--	--	--	--	--	--	--	--	--	--	--	11/15/1965	2,500	--	--
1967	--	--	--	--	--	--	--	--	--	--	--	--	--	--	11/4/1966	2,400	--	--
1968	--	--	--	--	--	--	--	--	--	--	--	--	--	--	--	--	--	--
1969	--	--	--	--	--	--	--	--	--	--	--	--	--	--	5/28/1969	2,940	--	--
1970	6/19/1970	--	--	--	--	--	--	--	--	--	--	--	--	--	6/10/1970	5,170	--	--
1971	--	--	--	--	--	--	--	--	--	--	--	--	--	--	6/28/1971	3,250	--	--
1972	--	--	--	--	--	--	--	--	--	--	--	--	--	--	9/21/1972	3,250	--	--
1973	--	--	--	--	--	--	--	--	--	--	--	--	--	--	11/18/1972	2,270	--	--
1974	--	--	--	--	--	--	--	--	--	--	--	--	--	--	6/25/1974	2,030	--	--
1975	--	--	--	--	--	--	--	--	--	--	--	--	--	--	10/13/1974	2,320	--	--
1976	6/9/1976	--	--	--	--	--	--	-56	70	75	-83	-123	-130	-93	10/21/1975	2,420	--	--
1977	--	--	--	--	--	--	--	--	--	--	--	--	--	--	10/12/1976	2,220	--	--
1978	--	--	--	--	--	--	--	--	--	--	--	--	--	--	3/15/1978	2,040	--	--
1979	--	--	--	--	--	--	--	--	--	--	--	--	--	--	10/9/1978	1,710	--	--
1980	9/4/1980	0	0	0	0	0	0	0	0	0	0	0	0	0	7/3/1980	1,960	--	--
1981	7/20/1981	0	0	0	0	0	0	0	0	0	0	0	0	0	6/10/1981	2,620	--	--
1982	--	--	--	--	--	--	--	--	--	--	--	--	--	--	6/28/1982	2,280	--	--
1983	--	--	--	--	--	--	--	--	--	--	--	--	--	--	11/19/1982	2,020	--	--
1984	7/31/1984	0	0	0	0	0	0	-46	0	0	44	0	0	0	11/14/1983	2,280	--	--
1985	--	--	--	--	--	--	--	--	--	--	--	--	--	--	11/21/1984	2,400	6/2/1985	2,190

Table 3. Lateral channel movement and annual peak streamflows for the Madison River, Montana.—Continued

[Negative value (-) indicates movement to the left bank (south), positive value indicates movement to the right bank (north). Abbreviations: +/-, plus or minus; ft, feet; USGS, U.S. Geological Survey; ft³/s, cubic feet per second. Symbol: -- data not available or not applicable]

| Water year | Date of photo-graphy | Channel movement (+/-30 feet) at or between indicated cross sections, between indicated date and date of previous aerial photograph (ft) | | | | | | | | | | | | | Annual peak streamflow at USGS streamflow-gaging station | | | |
| | | Spillway | | | | | | | | Downstream from spillway | | | | | Madison River below Hebgen Lake, near Grayling, Mont. (06038500) | | Madison River at Kirby Ranch, near Cameron, Mont. (06038800) | |
		Earth-quake Lake outlet / Cross section 1400	Cross section 1300	Cross section 1200	Cross section 1100	Cross section 1000	Cross section 900	Cross section 800	Cross section 700	Cross section 600	Between cross sections 600 and 500	Cross section 500	Between cross sections 500 and 400	Cross section 400	Date of streamflow	Stream-flow (ft³/s)	Date of streamflow	Stream-flow (ft³/s)
1986	6/12/1986	0	0	52	-71	68	56	52	0	47	330	110	370	200	6/5/1986	3,340	6/6/1986	5,000
1987	9/6/1987	0	0	0	0	0	0	0	40	0	0	0	0	0	11/8/1986	1,970	7/23/1987	1,790
1988	--	--	--	--	--	--	--	--	--	--	--	--	--	--	8/5/1988	1,430	5/17/1988	1,680
1989	--	--	--	--	--	--	--	--	--	--	--	--	--	--	12/13/1988	2,090	5/11/1989	1,870
1990	9/10/1990	0	0	0	0	0	0	0	0	0	0	0	0	0	11/14/1989	2,040	6/11/1990	2,380
1991	--	--	--	--	--	--	--	--	--	--	--	--	--	--	6/8/1991	2,620	6/8/1991	3,780
1992	7/29/1992	0	0	0	0	0	0	0	0	0	0	0	0	0	11/18/1991	1,680	7/5/1992	1,490
1993	--	--	--	--	--	--	--	--	--	--	--	--	--	--	5/27/1993	3,970	5/31/1993	5,030
1994	--	--	--	--	--	--	--	--	--	--	--	--	--	--	11/3/1993	2,260	5/29/1994	1,980
1995	8/12/1995	0	0	0	-38	0	-42	0	0	73	0	-76	-150	-40	6/11/1995	2,600	6/14/1995	3,950
1996	--	--	--	--	--	--	--	--	--	--	--	--	--	--	6/7/1996	3,880	6/7/1996	4,840
1997	--	--	--	--	--	--	--	--	--	--	--	--	--	--	6/12/1997	3,570	6/6/1997	4,700
1998	--	--	--	--	--	--	--	--	--	--	--	--	--	--	6/27/1998	2,860	6/26/1998	3,560
1999	--	--	--	--	--	--	--	--	--	--	--	--	--	--	6/13/1999	2,430	6/16/1999	3,340
2000	9/7/2000	0	0	0	0	0	0	0	0	0	94	0	63	-150	5/26/2000	1,750	5/29/2000	2,520
2001	--	--	--	--	--	--	--	--	--	--	--	--	--	--	7/9/2001	1,140	7/12/2001	1,330
2002	9/10/2002	0	0	0	0	0	0	0	0	0	0	0	0	0	7/16/2002	1,670	6/2/2002	2,050
2003	--	--	--	--	--	--	--	--	--	--	--	--	--	--	7/21/2003	1,890	5/30/2003	2,170
2004	--	--	--	--	--	--	--	--	--	--	--	--	--	--	7/7/2004	1,270	7/8/2004	1,490
2005	1/1/2005	0	0	-60	-73	0	-52	-55	0	0	0	0	65	0	6/15/2005	2,180	6/22/2005	2,720
2006	1/1/2006	0	0	0	0	0	0	0	0	0	0	0	0	0	5/25/2006	2,410	5/26/2006	3,450

[1] From U.S. Geological Survey (2008).

Figure 4.   Madison River downstream from Earthquake Lake, Montana. *A*, Looking upstream from cross section 1100, September 1971 [streamflow 400 cubic feet per second at Madison River below Hebgen Lake, near Grayling, Montana (06038500)]. *B*, Looking upstream from farther downstream and slightly south when compared to photograph *A*, September 2008 [streamflow 3,650 cubic feet per second at Madison River at Kirby Ranch near Cameron, Montana (06038800)].

Figure 5.   Madison River downstream from Earthquake Lake, Montana, looking downstream at cross section 800. *A*, September 1971, [streamflow 400 cubic feet per second at Madison River below Hebgen Lake, near Grayling, Montana (06038500)]. *B*, June 2006, [streamflow 1,040 cubic feet per second at Madison River at Kirby Ranch near Cameron, Montana (06038800)].

Right bank eroded between 1971 and 2006

Figure 6.   Madison River downstream from Earthquake Lake, Montana, looking downstream at cross section 600.

Lateral channel-movement and peak-flow data are shown in figure 8. Where more than one year lapsed between aerial photographs, it is not possible to discern whether the channel moved gradually or all in one year. It also is unclear whether the channel moved in response to one peak flow, to several peak flows, or to sustained flows.

Due to the narrow valley through the Madison Slide and the steep, high banks, the channel generally has laterally moved less through the spillway (fig. 8, cross sections 1400–700) than downstream from the spillway (fig. 8, cross sections 600–400). In addition, channel movement from about cross section 800 to cross section 700 (fig. 8) was less than the other portions of the spillway (cross section 1400–900) in 1986, 1995, and 2000. Movement from about cross section 800 to cross section 700 was less than the other spillway locations except for cross section 1100 in 2005. This subreach from about cross section 800 to cross section 700 is locally

known as the "knickpoint." A knickpoint is an abrupt drop-off, or increase in the longitudinal slope.

Data in figure 8 indicate that streamflows higher than the 3,500-ft³/s threshold were followed by lateral channel movement except from 1991 to 1992 and possibly from 1996 to 1997. Flows exceeded the threshold in 1996 and 1997, but no aerial photographs were available between 1995 and 2000; thus, aerial photography data from which to determine channel movement between the 1996 and 1997 high flows were unavailable. However, the stream moved laterally 120 to 150 ft between cross sections 500 and 600 during the relatively high streamflows in 1996 (Brent Mabbott, PPL-Montana, written commun., 2010). Moreover, the channel moved between 2002 and 2005 even though streamflows during that period were less than the 3,500-ft³/s threshold streamflow (fig. 8).

Figure 7. Madison River downstream from Earthquake Lake, Montana, upstream from cross section 800. *A*, September 1971 [streamflow 400 cubic feet per second at Madison River Hebgen Lake, near Grayling, Montana (06038500)]. *B*, June 2006 [streamflow 1,040 cubic feet per second at Madison River at Kirby Ranch near Cameron, Montana (06038800)].

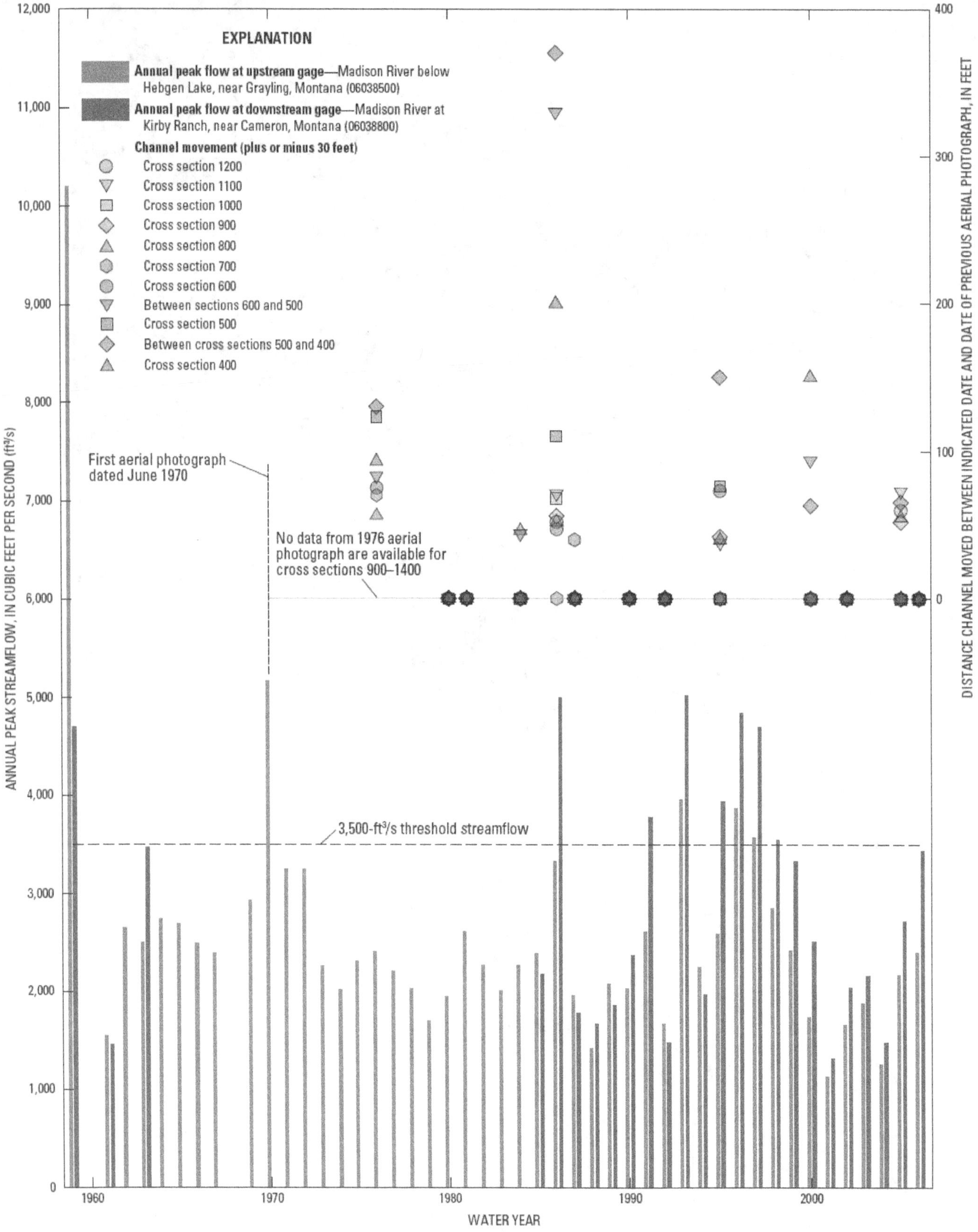

Figure 8.   Lateral channel movement for selected sites along the Madison River and annual peak streamflow for the Madison River, Montana.

Vertical Movement by Channel Incision and Aggradation

Between 1971 and 2006, the Madison River channel has aggraded and incised to varying degrees throughout the study area. Incision and aggradation are reflected in changes in thalweg and water-surface elevations.

Thalweg Elevations

Using survey notes from 1971 and survey data from 2006, the vertical changes in the channel thalweg can be determined by constructing longitudinal profiles from thalweg-elevation data for each cross section (fig. 9). As discussed in the section "Study Methods," the 1971 and 2006 thalweg elevations were measured at cross section 1400, but thalweg elevations for cross sections 1300–400 were estimated in the field. The estimated 2006 thalweg elevations were checked for reasonableness by using HEC-RAS calculations.

At the Earthquake Lake outlet (cross section 1400), the channel incised by about 4–5 ft. In addition, a knickpoint between cross sections 1000 and 900 that was present in the surveyed 1971 thalweg profile was smaller or no longer present in the surveyed 2006 thalweg profile (fig. 9). Foundation and Materials Consultants, Inc. (1972) reported that a "massive piece of rock" near cross section 1000 provided resistance to erosion. This rock might have moved downstream, or the channel could have moved to the side of the rock, causing the channel thalweg to lower by about 12 ft at cross section 1000.

The estimated thalweg surveyed in 2006 at cross section 700 appears to be about 7 ft higher than the thalweg estimated during the survey in 1971. This aggradation at cross section 700, combined with incision at cross section 600 (fig. 9), has resulted in a steeper thalweg slope between these two cross sections. Between cross sections 800 and 600, the Madison River channel is narrower and the water moves faster. The channel (about 300 ft upstream from cross section 700) generally has not moved laterally compared to the subreaches downstream and upstream (fig. A–9). The materials lining the channel bottom and sides of this subreach are larger and more resistant to erosion than the channel materials upstream and downstream. Car-sized boulders near cross section 700 were observed (fig.10) in 1971, 2006 and, 2008; these large boulders are depicted on the bed and banks in figure 10B. Erosion-resistant materials also are visible high above the river on each side of the channel. Hadley (1964) and U.S. Army Corps of Engineers (1972) describe a large dolomite outcrop or buttress between cross sections 700 and 800 high on the left bank (fig. 10A and 10B). The two reports also describe a 30-ft boulder that was deposited by the Madison Slide on the right bank, about 700 ft from the channel (fig. 10C). The subreach just downstream from cross section 700 to cross section 600 has been described as a "pivot point" where incision stops and deposition begins (Foundation and Materials Consultants, Inc., 1972).

At the downstream end of the study reach near cross section 400, the 2006 thalweg elevation is slightly higher than the 1971 thalweg elevation (fig. 9). The channel has migrated substantially between cross sections 600 and 400 (as discussed in the section "Lateral Movement").

Some of the decreases in thalweg elevations after 1971 could have been due to settlement of the Madison Slide material. Foundation and Materials Consultants, Inc. (1972) states that the Madison Slide material settled an average of 5 ft between 1959 and 1972. However, the settlement curve in the 1972 report projects that settling after 1972 would be much less than settling before 1972. Based on these data, and because no other information regarding Madison Slide settlement was available, settling of the materials after 1972 is assumed to be negligible for this study.

Water-Surface Elevations

Water-surface elevations are easier to survey than thalweg elevations in rivers like the Madison that are difficult to wade due to large depths and velocities. The water-surface profiles constructed from water-surface elevations surveyed along the Madison River in 1971 and 2006 include many more surveyed points than the 11 thalweg points from the cross-section surveys. Other water-surface profiles are available from Johnson and Omang (1972) and from project files. These water-surface profiles provide some information about channel changes from 1960–2006. However, water-surface profiles from different dates are difficult to compare because water-surface elevations change with streamflow and with the geometry of the channel.

Accordingly, the water-surface profiles from the 1971 and 2006 data are difficult to compare because streamflows were different during the two surveys (400 ft³/s at the upstream gage in 1971; 1,040 ft³/s at the downstream gage in 2006). Therefore, a water-surface profile was computed using HEC-RAS to represent water-surface elevations (referred to as the calculated 2006 water-surface profile in this report) for a streamflow of 400 ft³/s through the study reach for channel conditions in 2006 (fig. 11).

The water-surface elevation of the lake has decreased along with the elevation of the thalweg at the outlet since 1971. The lake water-surface elevation in 1971 was 6,387.5 ft (above NGVD 29) when streamflow at the upstream gage was 400 ft³/s (Johnson and Omang, 1972). At cross section 1400 (the outlet of Earthquake Lake), the calculated water-surface elevation for the 400 ft³/s streamflow in 2006 was 6,382.0 ft (above NGVD 29), indicating that the water surface of the lake (when Earthquake Lake outlet flows are 400 ft³/s) has decreased by 5.5 ft since 1971 because of channel incision at the Earthquake Lake outlet.

Comparisons of the water-surface profiles surveyed in 1960 and 1971 and the calculated 2006 water-surface profile indicate that the upper 2,500 ft of the study reach experienced the largest decrease in water-surface elevations since 1960, and the upper 1,500 ft of the study reach experienced the

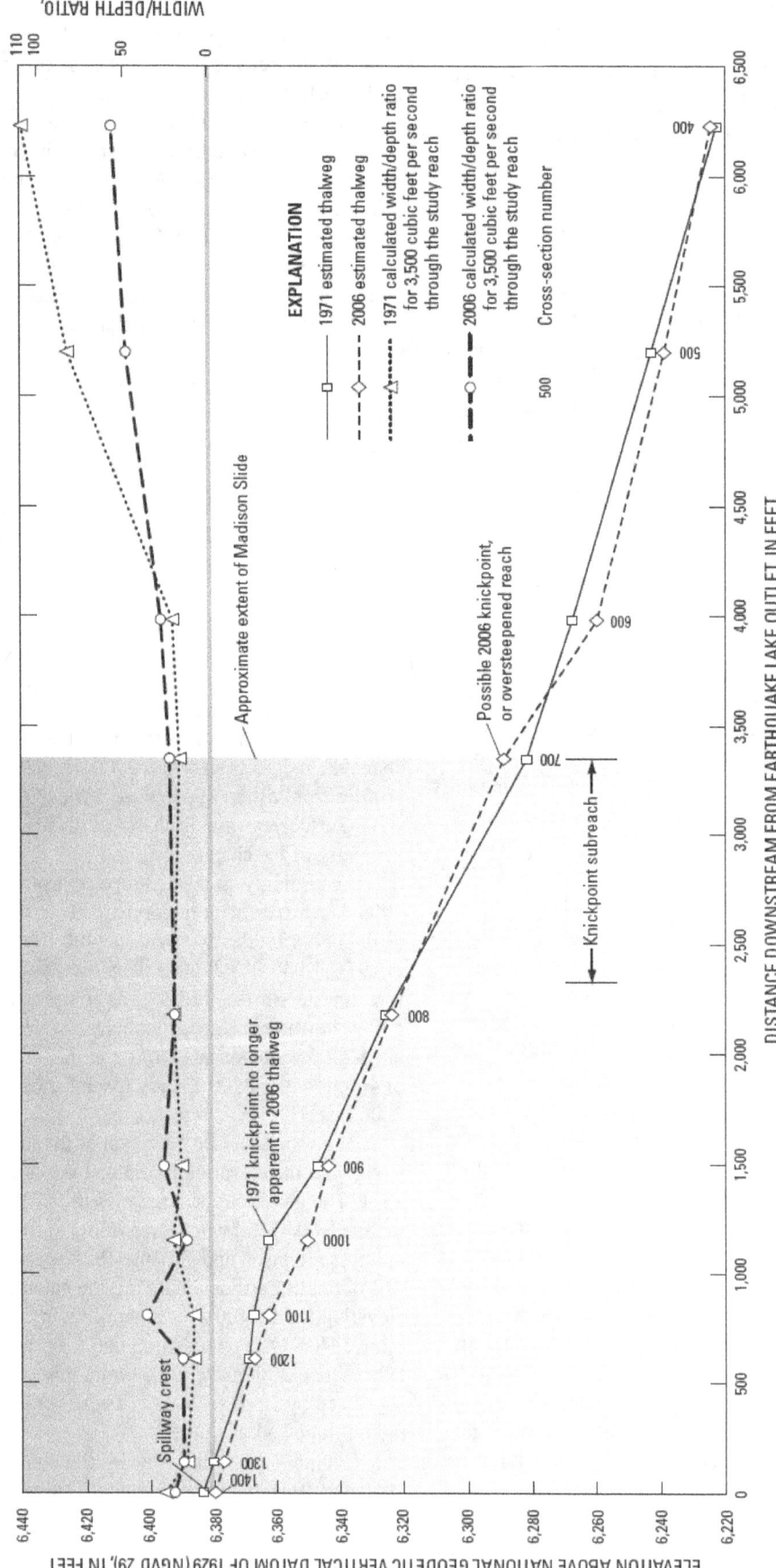

Figure 9.   Estimated thalweg profiles and calculated width/depth ratios of the Madison River downstream from Earthquake Lake, Montana.

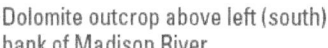

Dolomite outcrop above left (south) bank of Madison River

Large dolomite boulders on streambed and banks

Figure 10.   Erosion-resistant materials above the Madison River, downstream from Earthquake Lake, Montana. *A*, Dolomite outcrop above left bank of Madison River between cross sections 700 and 800, looking south from above road, August, 1959. *B*, Portion of same outcrop looking southwest from right bank of river, June, 2008. *C*, Large boulder above right bank between cross sections 700 and 800, September 1959.

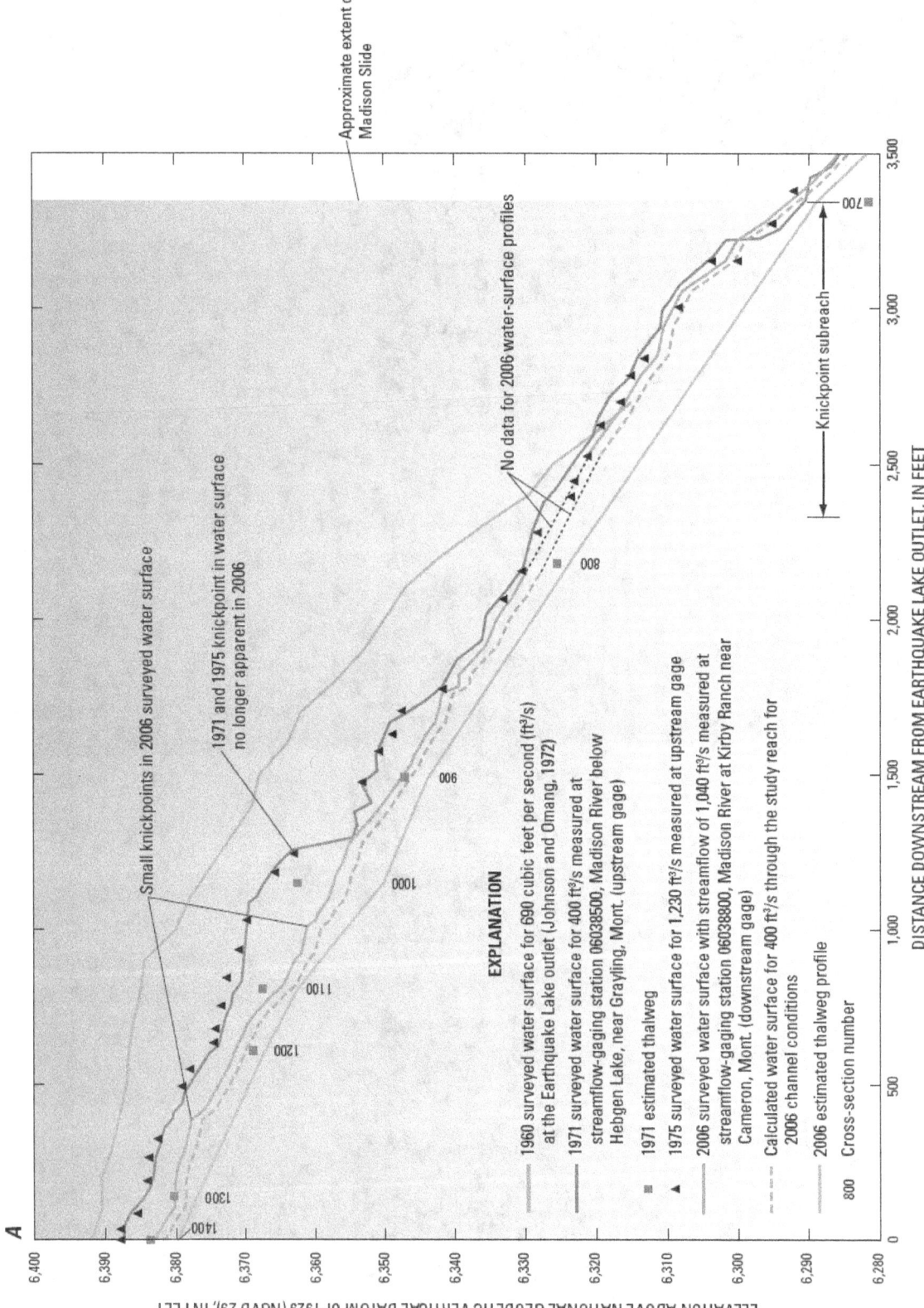

Figure 11. Surveyed water-surface profiles, calculated water-surface profile, and estimated thalweg profiles of the Madison River downstream from Earthquake Lake, Montana. *A*, Profiles from cross section 1400 to cross section 700. *B*, Profiles from cross section 700 to cross section 400.

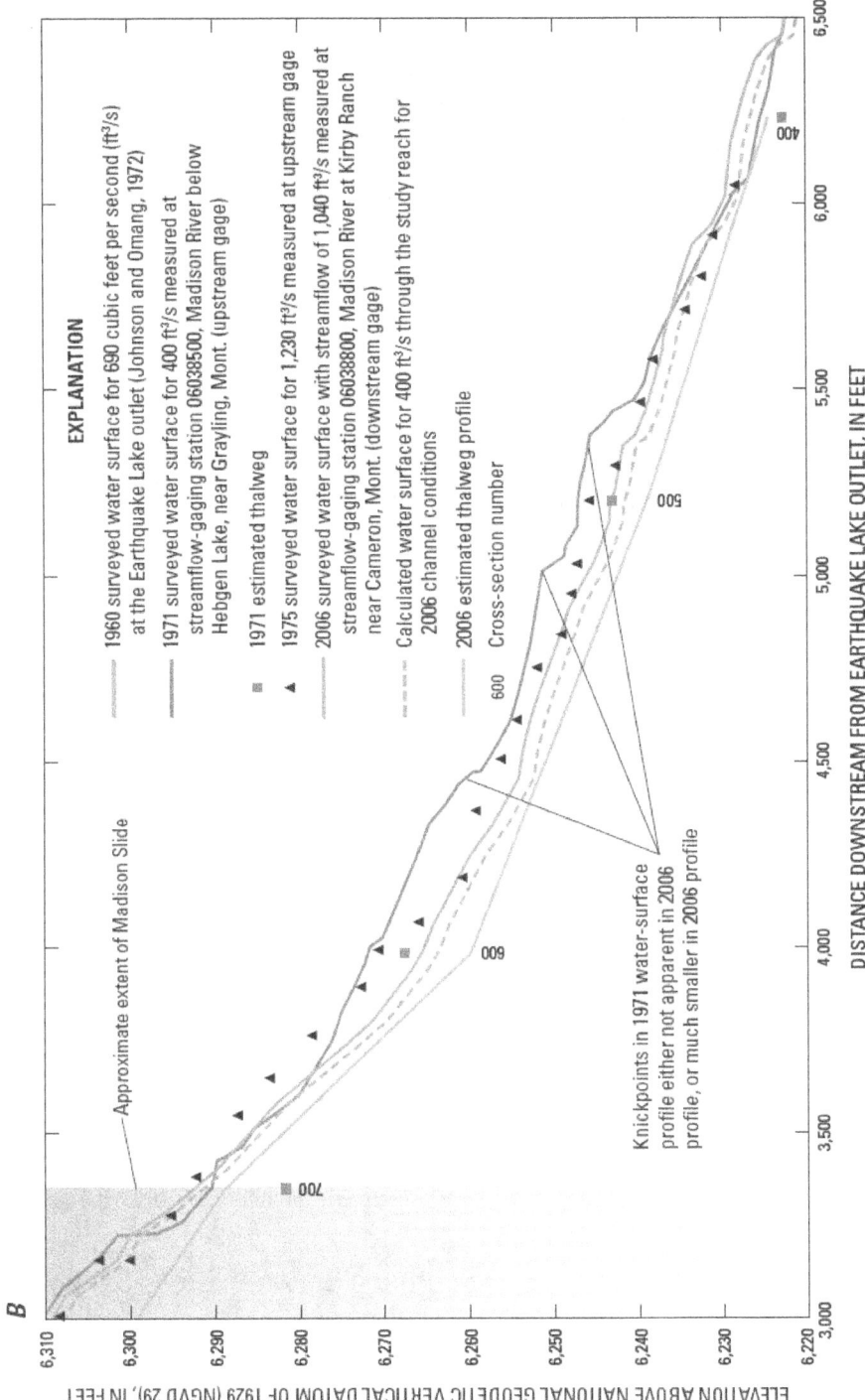

Figure 11. Surveyed water-surface profiles, calculated water-surface profile, and estimated thalweg profiles of the Madison River downstream from Earthquake Lake, Montana. *A*, Profiles from cross section 1400 to cross section 700. *B*, Profiles from cross section 700 to cross section 400.—Continued

largest decrease since 1971 (fig. 11). The water-surface elevation at cross section 1100 decreased by about 20 ft between 1960 and 2006. Most of this change occurred between 1960 and 1971; however, at cross section 1100 the water surface elevation decreased as much as 8 ft between 1975 and 2006.

The 1971 and 1975 water-surface profiles show a knickpoint downstream from cross section 1000. This knickpoint was not apparent in the surveyed 2006 water-surface profile, possibly due to the undercutting of one or more large boulders since the 1971 survey as discussed in the section on "Thalweg Elevations." Instead, smaller knickpoints are evident in the surveyed 2006 water-surface profile between cross sections 1300 and 1200 and between 1100 and 1000 (fig. 11).

Farther downstream, water-surface elevations decreased very little through the knickpoint subreach downstream from cross section 800 to cross section 700, where water surfaces differ by less than 2.5 ft from 1971 through 2006 (fig. 11*A*). As discussed in the section "Lateral Movement," the channel moved very little laterally through this subreach as well. However, for a short subreach near cross section 700, the calculated 2006 water-surface elevations are slightly higher than the 1971 water-surface elevations. This change corresponds to the aggradation in the same location between 1971 and 2006 as discussed in the section "Thalweg Elevations."

At cross section 600 (fig. 11*B*), the calculated 2006 water-surface elevation is more than 8 ft lower than the surveyed 1971 water-surface elevation. The surveyed 2006 water-surface elevation (streamflow of 1,040 ft³/s at the downstream gage) is almost 6 ft lower than the surveyed 1975 water-surface elevation (streamflow of 1,230 ft³/s at the upstream gage). These comparisons indicate that much of the decrease in water surfaces at this location occurred after 1975.

Between cross section 600 and cross section 500, the surveyed 1971 water-surface elevation and the calculated 2006 water-surface elevations differences ranged from about 5 to 8 ft. For this same subreach the differences between the surveyed 1975 water-surface elevation and the surveyed 2006 water surface elevation ranged from about 1 to 3 ft, indicating that most of the decrease in water surfaces in the reach between cross sections 600 and 500 occurred before 1975.

Downstream from cross section 500, the surveyed 1971 water-surface elevations become closer to the calculated 2006 water-surface elevations, and the surveyed 1975 water-surface elevations become closer to the surveyed 2006 water-surface elevations, indicating that less incision occurred through this part of the channel. Some aggradation is apparent just upstream from cross sections 400, where the calculated 2006 water-surface elevations are slightly higher than the surveyed 1971 water-surface elevations.

Lateral and Vertical Movement by Channel Subreach

The lateral and vertical channel movement at Madison River subreaches between 1971 and 2006 can be determined from the cross sections in figure 12 and from the width/depth ratios (calculated for a 3,500-ft³/s streamflow through the study reach) in figure 9. Changes in width/depth ratios integrate both vertical and lateral channel movement. For example, an increased width/depth ratio indicates a channel that is widening and/or getting shallower and a decreased width/depth ratio indicates a channel that is narrowing and/or becoming deeper.

Subreach Between Cross Sections 1400 and 900

In this subreach that extends from the outlet of Earthquake Lake through the upper one-third of the spillway, between 1971 and 2006 the Madison River (generally) eroded into the left and right banks and incised (fig. 4, fig. 12, and appendix 1). The channel shifted left at cross section 1300, right at cross section 1200, left at cross section 1100, and right again at 1000. Large amounts of bank material probably collapsed into the channel and likely were transported downstream. Instead of aggrading, the channel incised about 5 ft at cross section 1400, 4 ft at cross section 1300, 2 ft at cross section 1200, 4 ft at cross section 1100, and 12 ft at cross section 1000 (figs. 9, 11, and 12).

The channel shape (fig. 12) and width/depth ratios (fig. 9) are fairly similar for cross sections 1400 through 1200, and had changed little between 1971 and 2006. However, the width/depth ratio at cross section 1100 (figs. 4 and 9) increased more than 300 percent between 1971 and 2006 and also is larger than the width/depth ratios at cross sections 1200 and 1000. This increase is a result of the channel eroding into the left and right banks, (figs. 4, 12, A–4, A–6, and A–8).

The knickpoint in the 1971 thalweg profile between cross sections 1000 and 900 is not apparent in the 2006 thalweg profile (figs. 9 and 11). The large knickpoint in the water-surface profile that was surveyed in 1971 at close to the same location as the thalweg knickpoint (fig. 11) is not apparent in the surveyed 2006 water-surface profile. Instead, smaller knickpoints are evident in the surveyed 2006 water-surface profile between cross sections 1300 and 1200 and between 1100 and 1000.

Subreach Between Cross Sections 900 and 600

In this subreach that extends from the middle of the spillway to just downstream from the Madison Slide, less lateral and vertical movement was detected between 1971 and 2006 than in the upstream and downstream subreaches. The channel has shifted into the right bank (figs. 12 and A–9). The channel aggraded at cross section 700 but incised at cross section 600, resulting in a flatter thalweg slope between cross sections 800 and 700 and a steeper thalweg slope between cross sections

700 and 600 (fig. 9). Additionally, the width/depth ratios increased by 5–10 ft/ft at cross sections 900, 700, and 600 but did not change at cross section 800, even though the channel at cross section 800 shifted into the right bank between 1971 and 2006 (figs. 5 and 12). Along the knickpoint portion of the subreach, generally from cross section 800 to cross section 700, the channel has moved very little laterally or vertically, perhaps because of large, erosion-resistant rocks in that area as discussed in the "Thalweg Elevations" section.

Subreach Between Cross Sections 600 and 400

In this subreach that begins just below the spillway, the channel moved considerably laterally and vertically at cross sections 600 and 500, as the river deposited large amounts of material into the channel, eroded into the right bank, and then incised into a new channel, ultimately lowering the thalweg (figs. 9, 12, and A–9). At cross section 400, the river deposited material into the right side of the 1971 channel and currently (2006) occupies the left side of the 1971 channel, slightly raising the thalweg.

The channel downstream from the spillway has higher width/depth ratios than the upstream channel (fig. 9). By 2006, the width/depth ratios at cross sections 500 and 400 had decreased by about 30 to 50 ft/ft since 1971 (fig. 9). At these cross sections, the channel seems to be changing from a braided channel to a single meandering channel (fig. 12). However, this subreach could again become more braided if large amounts of material are eroded from the steep upstream streambanks and deposited through this area.

Vertical Channel Changes near Raynolds Pass Bridge

Three cross sections near Raynolds Pass Bridge about 3 mi downstream from Earthquake Lake (fig. 2) were surveyed in 1971 and then resurveyed in 2006 to determine if materials eroded from the spillway were being deposited near the bridge. Comparison of the cross sections from the two surveys (1971 and 2006) indicates that the channel was as much as 1.4 ft lower in some parts of cross sections 100 and 200 downstream from the bridge in 1971 than 2006 (fig. 13). Additionally, the channel at one location in cross section 300 was as much as 1.9 ft higher in the 2006 cross section compared to the 1971 cross section. These differences between the two surveys were local and could represent a few rocks or depressions in the bed. Also at cross section 300, the right bank was about 5 ft lower in the 2006 survey than the 1971 survey. This difference between the right bank elevations from the 1971 and 2006 surveys could be due to erosion along the right bank just downstream from the bridge or due to the two surveys being in slightly different locations. Overall, it does not appear that materials eroded from the spillway are causing aggradation in this subreach.

Limitations of the Estimates of Lateral and Vertical Channel Movement

Channel movement was determined from aerial photographs and sparse survey data. A relation between streamflow and channel movement is difficult to determine because more than a year passed between most of the aerial photographs and more than 30 years passed between the most recent surveys. Resurveying cross sections and water-surface elevations more frequently (either annually or after high streamflows) could better define the relation between streamflow and lateral and vertical channel movement.

Potential for Bed-Material Movement

The ability of a river to move its bed material is a function of streamflow, energy slope, flow depth, and bed-material characteristics (Shields, 1936). To estimate the potential for bed-material movement for selected streamflows along the Madison River, materials from in and near the channel were measured and shear stresses for selected streamflows were calculated. Though several streamflows were analyzed, only the 3,500-ft^3/s threshold streamflow is discussed in detail.

Characteristics of Materials In and Near the Madison River Channel

Hadley (1964) observed that most of the surface of the Madison Slide consisted of angular blocks of gneiss, schist, and dolomite. The gneiss fragments were 6 to 60 inches (in.) long, and the schist fragments were 1 to 12 in. long. Beneath the top few feet of the Madison Slide debris, smaller rock fragments, as well as sand-, silt-, and clay-sized material were present when the USACE excavated the spillway. The Madison Slide debris was estimated to be up to 220 ft deep between cross sections 700 and 800 (fig. 2) and was estimated to thin gradually at the upstream and downstream boundaries of the Madison Slide (Hadley, 1964). A drill log showed that boulders and cobbles existed down to at least the base of the drill hole (50 ft below the surface) on the right bank between cross sections 800 and 900 (Foundation and Materials Consultants, Inc., 1972). The right bank is about 50 ft above the bed in this subreach; thus, the base of the drill hole probably was at or slightly above the elevation of the thalweg.

Data for particle sizes measured in and near the channel in 2006 and 2008, as well as particle sizes measured by the USACE in 1959 and in 1970 (U.S. Army Corps of Engineers, 1972), are summarized in table 4 and figure 14. The D_{50} for all of the measurements (not including the rough visual estimate for the subreach between cross sections 700 and 800) ranged from 3.3 to 170 mm. The largest measured median particle sizes (D_{50} equal to 170 mm) were collected on the surface of the bed at the Earthquake Lake outlet (between cross sections

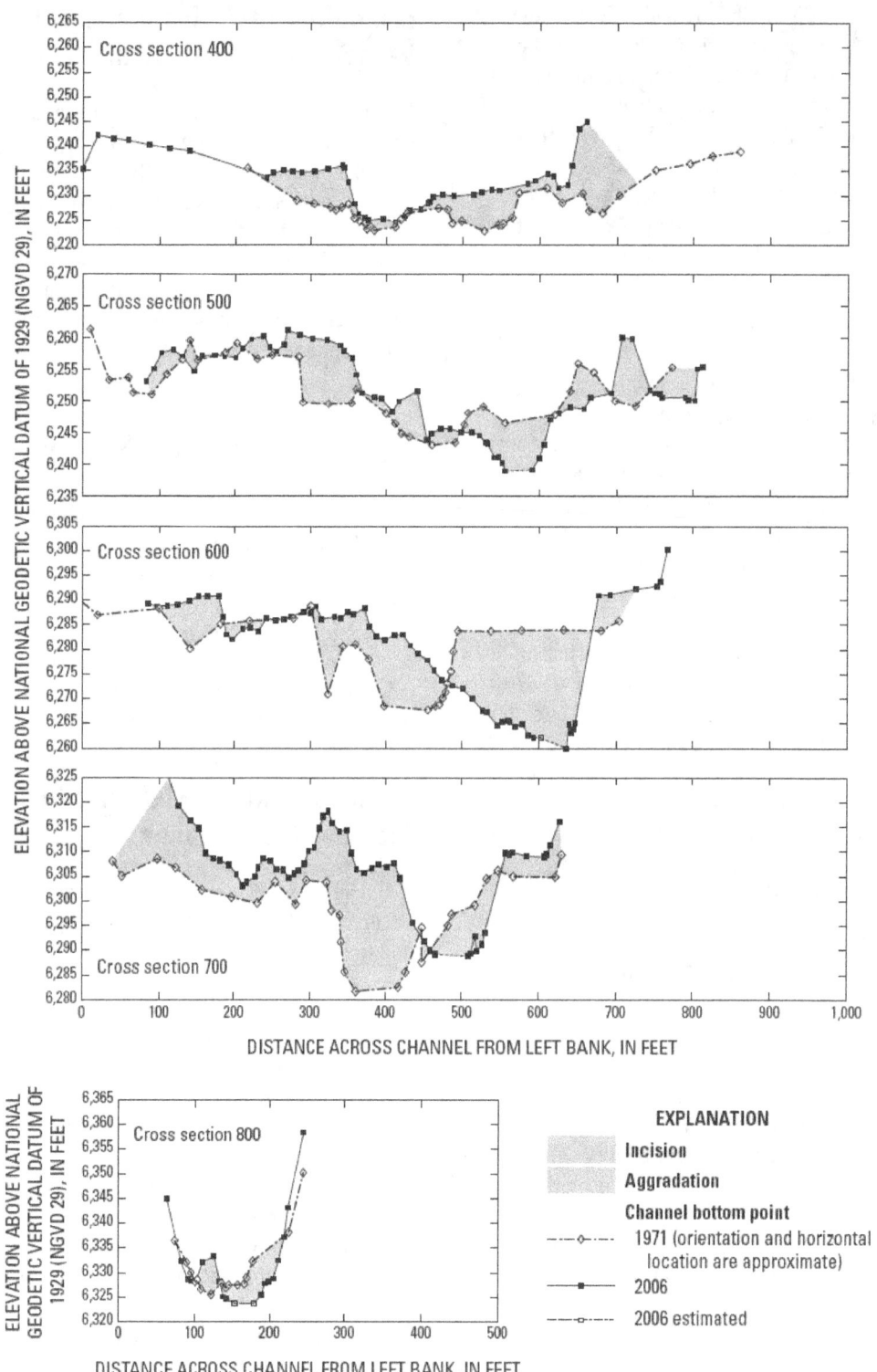

Figure 12.   Lateral migration, incision, and aggradation of the Madison River channel downstream from Earthquake Lake, Montana between 1971 and 2006.

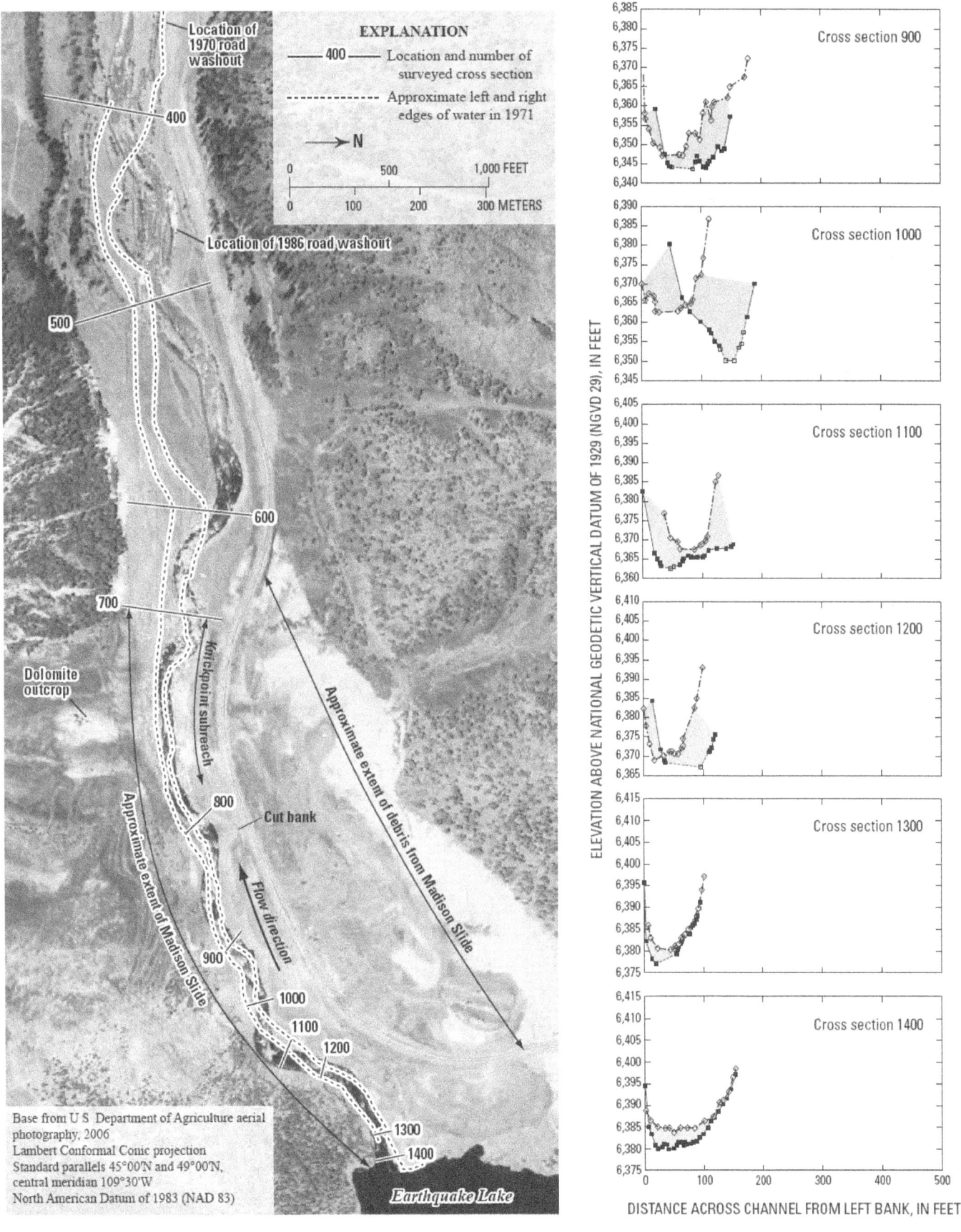

Figure 12. Lateral migration, incision, and aggradation of the Madison River channel downstream from Earthquake Lake, Montana between 1971 and 2006.—Continued

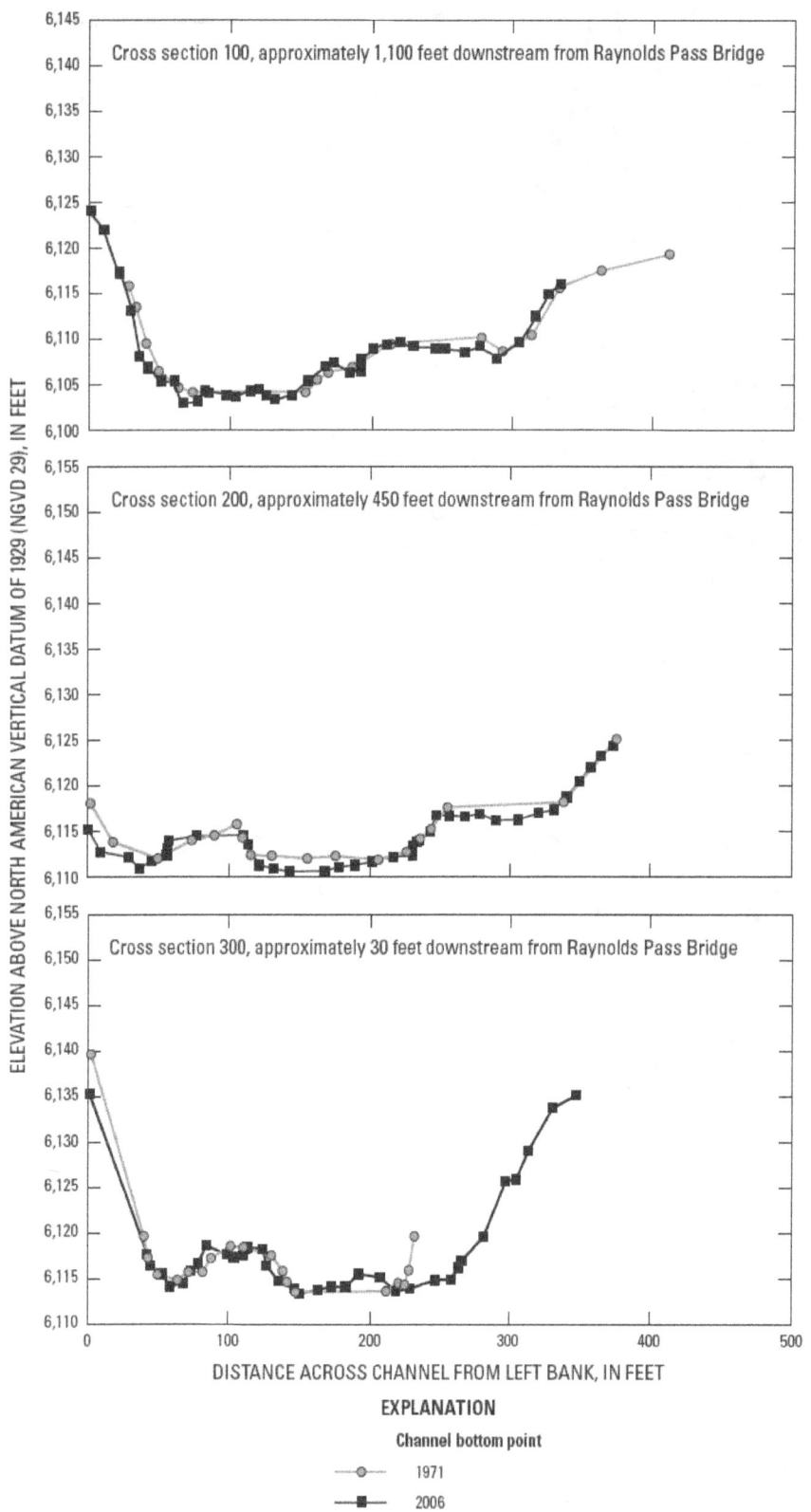

Figure 13. Cross sections 100, 200, and 300, from 1971 and 2006 surveys on the Madison River near Raynolds Pass Bridge downstream from Earthquake Lake, Montana.

1300 and 1400). However, larger particle sizes exist throughout the study reach where the deepest parts of the channel could not be waded or sampled; car-sized boulders near cross section 700 were observed in 1971, 2006 and, 2008. Additionally, bed-material samples 4, 6, and 7 (fig. 14) and the terrace material sample 5 were larger than the other measured materials. The presence of these larger bed and terrace materials probably indicates bed armoring as streamflows have washed finer material downstream.

The gradation coefficient, calculated as the square root of the ratio of D_{84}/D_{16} is a measure of the variability of the sediment-size distribution and provides some indication of gradation. For instance, if the gradation coefficient is about 1, the sediment is poorly graded and thus composed of material of similar sizes. The gradation coefficient was 1.7 to 2.2 for the bed surface, 2.2 for the terrace surface, and 4.6 to 6.5 for the materials sampled from the banks and the gravel bar (table 4). Unlike the pebble counts for the bed and terrace surfaces, the samples from the banks and the gravel bar included some materials below the surface. The bed and terrace surface materials are more poorly graded than the material on and below the surface on the channel banks and on the gravel bar, probably because of armoring of the bed.

Shear Stress and Potential for Bed-Material Movement

Boundary-shear stress is the force per unit area that a river exerts on its bed in the direction of flow (Dingman, 2009). The critical shear stress is the shear stress required to initiate movement of sediment of a specific size from the bed (Dingman, 2009). If the boundary-shear stress is larger than the critical shear stress for a given streamflow, the bed material is likely to move, potentially resulting in channel adjustments (Elliott, 2002).

Boundary-Shear Stress

Mean boundary-shear stress can be approximated by the du Bois equation (U.S. Army Corps of Engineers, 2008b, p. 12–29):

$$\tau_o = \gamma R S \qquad (3)$$

where

τ_o	is the mean boundary-shear stress, in pounds per square foot;
γ	is the specific weight of water (62.4 pounds per cubic foot);
R	is the hydraulic radius of the stream, or the cross-sectional area divided by the wetted perimeter, in feet; and
S	is the energy slope, in feet per feet.

The mean boundary-shear stress and hydraulic geometry variables (cross-sectional area, hydraulic radius, and energy slope) were calculated for several streamflows at the surveyed cross sections by using HEC-RAS (table 5). Mean boundary-shear stress for the 3,500-ft³/s threshold streamflow at cross section 400 is shown in figure 15. Also shown in figure 15 are the point boundary-shear stresses, which are calculated by substituting streamflow depth for the hydraulic radius in equation 3 at several locations across the cross section, to illustrate how the point boundary-shear stresses can vary across the channel. The mean boundary-shear stresses are less than the point boundary-shear stress at the deepest parts of the channel but are greater than the point boundary-shear stress along the sides of the channel.

The mean boundary-shear stresses vary longitudinally along the Madison River and generally increase with stream-flow (fig. 16). Mean boundary-shear stresses generally are higher at cross sections where the thalweg and water-surface slopes steepen because the mean boundary-shear stress is directly proportional to energy slope (equation 3), and the energy slope usually increases as the thalweg and water-surface slopes increase. Mean boundary-shear stresses also increase proportionally to depth and velocity (Dingman, 2009; Elliott, 2002). Mean boundary-shear stresses are high at cross section 700 (fig. 16B) where the steepest thalweg and water-surface slopes in the study reach occur (figs. 9 and 11B). Shear stresses are lower downstream from the spillway (near cross sections 600 to 400), where thalweg and water-surface slopes are flatter than the spillway. Therefore, many of the larger bed materials that could be entrained upstream are likely to be deposited through this subreach downstream from the spillway. This projected deposition is consistent with the thalweg and water-surface profile changes since 1971 and with historical observations (U.S. Army Corps of Engineers, 1972; Foundation and Materials Consultants, Inc., 1972).

Critical Shear Stress

Many investigations (Elliott, 2002; Elliott and Hammack, 2000; Heitmuller and Asquith, 2008) have used the Shields (1936) equation to estimate the critical shear stress for movement of the D_{50} particle size:

$$\tau_c = \tau_c^* \, (\gamma_s - \gamma) \, D_{50} \qquad (4)$$

where

τ_c	is the critical shear stress, in pounds per square foot;
τ_c^*	is the dimensionless critical shear stress, or Shields parameter;
γ_s	is the specific weight of sediment, assumed to be 2.65 times the specific weight of water, in pounds per cubic foot;
γ	is the specific weight of water (62.4 pound per cubic foot); and
D_{50}	is the median particle size, in feet.

Although equation 4 includes a variable for the D_{50} particle size, for this study critical shear stresses were calculated for the larger particle sizes (D_{65} and D_{84}) as well as the D_{50}. Larger materials in a bed can shield the smaller particles from flow, or the smaller particles can be removed from the bed leaving a coarser, armored bed. Consequently, a cobble- or boulder-bedded river like the Madison can be considered stable until the larger bed materials are in motion (Julien, 1998). For clarity, only the critical shear stresses for the D_{50} and D_{84} particle sizes are discussed in detail in this report.

Use of equation 4 requires an estimated or calculated dimensionless critical shear stress or Shields parameter. Shields parameter values ranging from 0.01 to 0.11 have been used for estimating particle motion (Elliott, 2002; Mueller and others, 2005). Elliott and Hammack (2000) determined from onsite observations of sediment movement that a value of 0.03 for the Shields parameter was appropriate for estimating movement of material from an alluvial bar along the Gunnison River in the Black Canyon, Colo. Elliott (2002) also used a Shields parameter value of 0.03 for estimating particle motion on the Roaring Fork River in Colo., which is a coarse-bed stream with sediment sizes in the same range as the Madison River. However, because the materials lining the spillway and the channel downstream from the spillway (cross sections 1400 to 400) were deposited by the Madison Slide, they have not been worn into smooth rounded shapes typical of bed material in the Gunnison and Roaring Fork Rivers, nor have they been reworked by the river over a long time (Hadley, 1964; figs. 3–7, this report). The bed materials in this part of the Madison River are more angular, which could result in a larger Shields parameter value (Julien, 1998).

Table 4.   Sediment-size characteristics and calculated critical shear stresses for materials in and near the Madison River downstream from Earthquake Lake, Montana.

[Horizontal coordinate information is referenced to the North American Datum of 1983 (NAD 83). Abbreviations: D_{xx}, particle size for which xx percent of material is finer; σ_g, gradation coefficient, which equals the square root of the ratio of D_{84} to D_{16}; $\tau_c(D_{xx})$ critical shear stress for given particle size; mm, millimeters; lb/ft^2, pounds per square foot; USGS, U.S. Geological Survey; ft, feet; USACE, U.S. Army Corps of Engineers. Symbol: -- data not available]

Collecting agency	Sample number	Year	Method	Approximate easting[1]	Approximate northing[1]	Description
USGS	1	2008	Sieve analysis	111°26′31″W	44°49′36″N	Gravel bar along right side of channel between cross sections 500 and 400
USGS	2	2008	Sieve analysis	111°27′8″W	44°49′38″N	Right bank above high water mark near cross section 600, along outside bend[3]
USGS	3	2008	Sieve analysis	111°25′27″W	44°49′47″N	Right bank between cross sections 1300 and 1200
USGS	4	2006	Pebble count[1,4]	111°25′24″W	44°49′47″N	Bed near spillway between cross sections 1400 and 1300
USGS	5	2006	Pebble count	111°26′35″W	44°49′34″N	Terrace on right bank 50 ft upstream from cross section 400
USGS	6	2006	Pebble count[1,5]	111°29′9″W	44°49′34″N	Bed between cross sections 300 and 100, near Raynolds Pass Bridge
USGS	7	2006	Pebble count[1,4]	111°26′33″W	44°49′33″N	Bed between cross sections 500 and 400
USGS	8	2006	Rough visual estimate[6]	--	--	Bed between cross sections 800 and 700
USACE	1	1959	Sieve analysis	--	--	Spillway, obtained during excavation, exact location unknown
USACE	1	1970	Sieve analysis	--	--	Mid part of alluvial fan, exact location unknown

[1] Pebble count samples covered large area of bed, location listed is in vicinity of sample area.

[2] Sediment-size distribution calculated by weight for sieve analysis, by number of particles for pebble-count analysis.

[3] Sample location was 4 feet above the water surface, just above where person was standing in figure 6.

[4] Left and center parts of channel unwadeable. Sampled the right part of the channel bed, which extended into the channel approximately 25 percent of distance across the channel.

[5] Center part of the channel unwadable. Sampled the left and right parts of the channel bed, which each extended into the channel approximately 25 percent of distance across the channel.

[6] Not sampled or measured.

Because this study did not include observations of bed-material movement from which to estimate the Shields parameter, a range of values for critical shear stress (τ_c) was estimated using information from three investigations. First, critical shear stress was calculated using a Shields parameter of 0.04 for a lower bound because this value was used by the USACE for their investigations along the Madison River (U.S. Army Corps of Engineers, 1972). Then, based on work by Wilcock and McArdell (1993), critical shear stress was calculated using a Shields parameter of 0.08 for an upper bound. Wilcock and McArdell (1993) showed that complete motion, where enough material is moving to cause incision of the bed, occurs at about twice the critical shear stress (equivalent to using a Shields parameter of 0.08). Lastly, Shields parameters were calculated as a function of particle shape and size (variable Shields parameters) as described by Julien (1998). Resulting variable Shields parameter values ranged from 0.04 to 0.06.

Cross Sections 500–400, Downstream from Spillway

Between cross sections 500 and 400 downstream from the spillway, the right part of the channel bed was sampled using the pebble-count method (table 4). The critical shear stresses calculated using the Shields parameter (0.04) and using the variable Shields parameter (0.04–0.06) for the D_{50} particle size are both smaller than both the mean boundary-shear stress and the point boundary-shear stress calculated

Table 4.   Sediment-size characteristics and calculated critical shear stresses for materials in and near the Madison River downstream from Earthquake Lake, Montana.—Continued

[Horizontal coordinate information is referenced to the North American Datum of 1983 (NAD 83). Abbreviations: D_{xx}, particle size for which xx percent of material is finer; σ_g, gradation coefficient, which equals the square root of the ratio of D_{84} to D_{16}; $\tau_c(D_{xx})$ critical shear stress for given particle size; mm, millimeters; lb/ft^2, pounds per square foot; USGS, U.S. Geological Survey; ft, feet; USACE, U.S. Army Corps of Engineers. Symbol: -- data not available]

Particle size for which indicated percentage of bed or bank material is finer[2]				Gradation coefficient	Critical shear stress for indicated particle size, calculated using Shields parameter =0.04			Critical shear stress for indicated particle size, calculated using variable Shields parameter (0.04–0.06) from Julien (1998)		
D_{16} (mm)	D_{50} (mm)	D_{65} (mm)	D_{84} (mm)	σ_g	$\tau_c(D_{50})$ (lb/ft^2)	$\tau_c(D_{65})$ (lb/ft^2)	$\tau_c(D_{84})$ (lb/ft^2)	$\tau_c(D_{50})$ (lb/ft^2)	$\tau_c(D_{65})$ (lb/ft^2)	$\tau_c(D_{84})$ (lb/ft^2)
3.7	18	33	78	4.6	0.24	0.45	1.06	0.26	0.51	1.33
1.0	6.2	13	42	6.4	.084	.18	.56	.080	.18	.65
2.3	22	55	95	6.5	.29	.74	1.3	.37	.94	1.7
110	170	200	300	1.7	2.3	2.7	4.1	3.1	3.7	5.6
32	90	130	160	2.2	1.2	1.8	2.2	1.4	2.2	2.7
38	83	120	180	2.2	1.1	1.6	2.4	1.3	1.9	2.9
64	150	180	280	2.1	2.0	2.4	3.8	2.6	3.1	4.9
--	1,000	--	--	--	14	--	--	19	--	--
.50	3.3	6.0	11	4.7	.045	.081	.15	.043	.085	.16
1.1	4.3	7.0	16	3.8	.058	.094	.22	.059	.099	.25

using equation 3 for cross section 400 for the 3,500-ft^3/s threshold streamflow (figs. 15 and 16B, table 5). This comparison indicates that some of the D_{50} particle sizes along the right side of the bed near cross section 400 could move at the 3,500-ft^3/s threshold streamflow. However, the critical shear stress for the D_{50} particle size calculated using the Shields parameter of 0.08 is larger than both the mean boundary-shear stress and the point boundary-shear stress, indicating that movement of all of the D_{50} particle sizes on the bed is unlikely at the 3,500-ft^3/s threshold streamflow.

The critical shear stresses for the D_{84} particle size calculated using the Shields parameter of 0.04, the variable Shields parameter, and the Shields parameter of 0.08 are all larger than both the mean boundary-shear stress and the point boundary-shear stress calculated for the 3,500-ft^3/s threshold streamflow, indicating that the larger size fractions along the bed near cross section 400 are not likely to move at the 3,500-ft^3/s threshold streamflow. This lack of movement for the larger particles could lead to further coarsening or armoring of the bed if the D_{50} and smaller sizes are removed from the bed and transported downstream. However, these smaller particles could be replenished by particles eroded from the steep banks upstream.

In summary, some of the D_{50} particle sizes along the right side of the bed between cross sections 500 and 400 could be moved by the 3,500-ft^3/s threshold streamflow. However, the D_{84} particle sizes probably would not move.

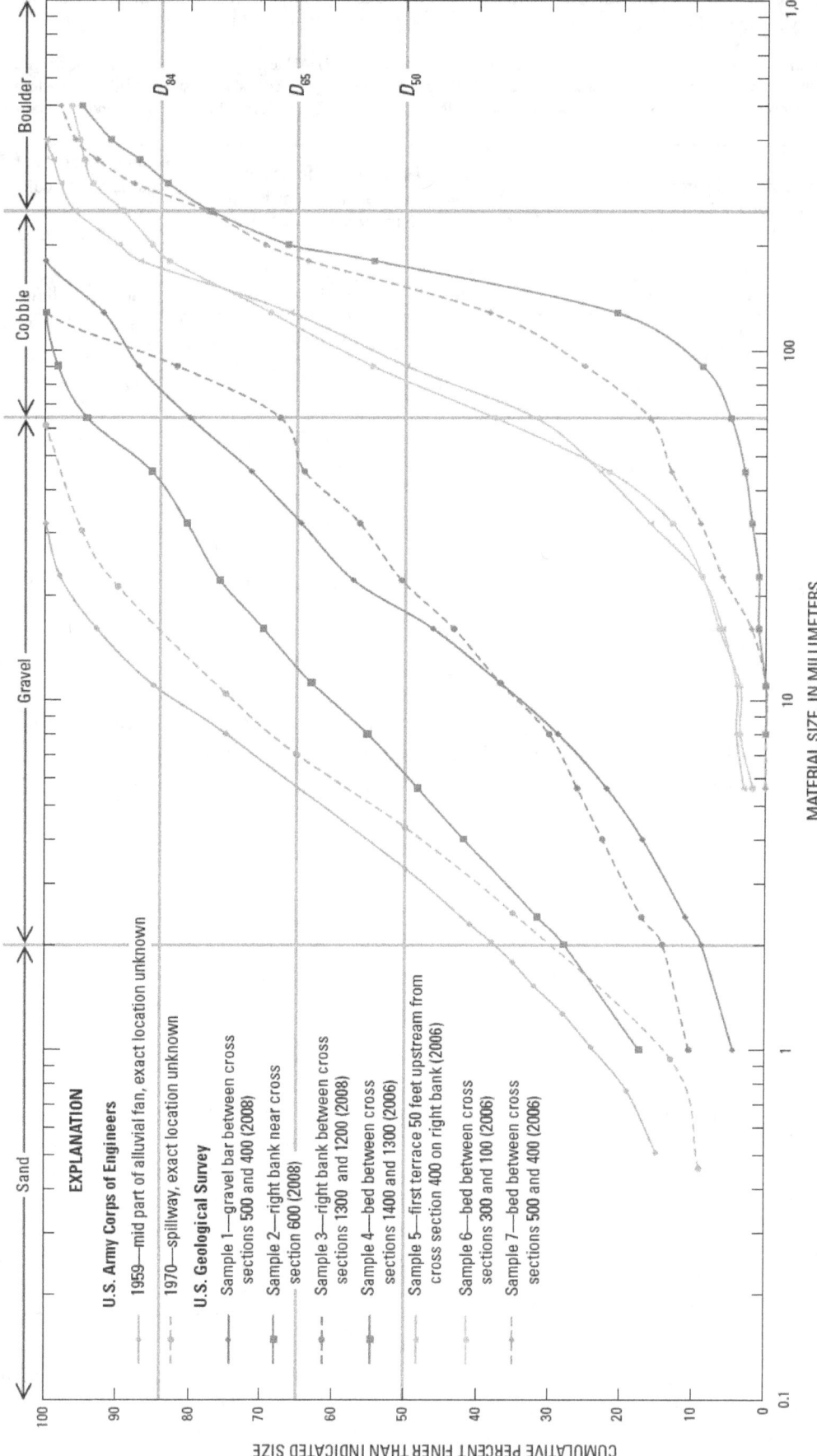

Figure 14.   Distribution of particle sizes of material in and near the Madison River downstream from Earthquake Lake, Montana.

Table 5. Calculated hydraulic characteristics for selected cross sections on the Madison River downstream from Earthquake Lake, Montana.

[Abbreviations: ft, feet; ; ft², square feet; ft/ft, foot per foot; lb/ft² pounds per square foot; ft³/s, cubic feet per second]

Cross-section number	Distance downstream from Earthquake Lake outlet (ft)	Mannings roughness coefficient (dimensionless)	Cross-sectional area[1] (ft²)	Hydraulic radius[1] (ft)	Energy slope[1] (ft/ft)	Mean boundary-shear stress[1] (lb/ft²)
Streamflow through the study reach at the time of the survey (2006) 1,040 ft³/s						
1400	0	0.055	255	2.7	0.006	1.0
1300	140	.080	143	2.6	.045	7.3
700	3,347	.110	169	2.2	.077	11
500	5,200	.080	238	3.2	.013	2.6
400	6,232	.075	232	2.4	.017	2.5
2,500 ft³/s						
1400	0	0.055	454	4.3	0.005	1.4
1300	140	.080	273	4.1	.034	8.7
700	3,347	.110	276	3.1	.092	18
500	5,200	.080	421	3.1	.013	2.5
400	6,232	.075	397	3.1	.017	3.3
3,000 ft³/s						
1400	0	0.055	518	4.7	0.005	1.5
1300	140	.080	314	4.4	.032	8.8
700	3,347	.110	300	3.4	.10	21
500	5,200	.080	488	3.0	.014	2.6
400	6,232	.075	473	2.8	.016	2.8
3,500 ft³/s						
1400	0	0.055	534	5.1	0.005	1.6
1300	140	.080	325	4.5	.030	8.4
700	3,347	.110	312	3.5	.12	26
500	5,200	.080	440	3.3	.015	3.1
400	6,232	.075	480	3.1	.015	2.9
4,000 ft³/s						
1400	0	0.055	641	5.4	0.005	1.7
1300	140	.080	396	4.9	.029	8.9
700	3,347	.110	352	3.8	.11	26
500	5,200	.080	602	3.6	.015	3.4
400	6,232	.075	624	3.1	.014	2.7
6,000 ft³/s						
1400	0	0.055	870	6.7	0.004	1.8
1300	140	.080	541	6.0	.026	9.7
700	3,347	.110	477	4.7	.10	29
500	5,200	.080	799	4.5	.017	4.8
400	6,232	.075	902	3.5	.014	3.1

[1]Calculated using HEC-RAS (U.S. Army Corps of Engineers, 2008a, b, c).

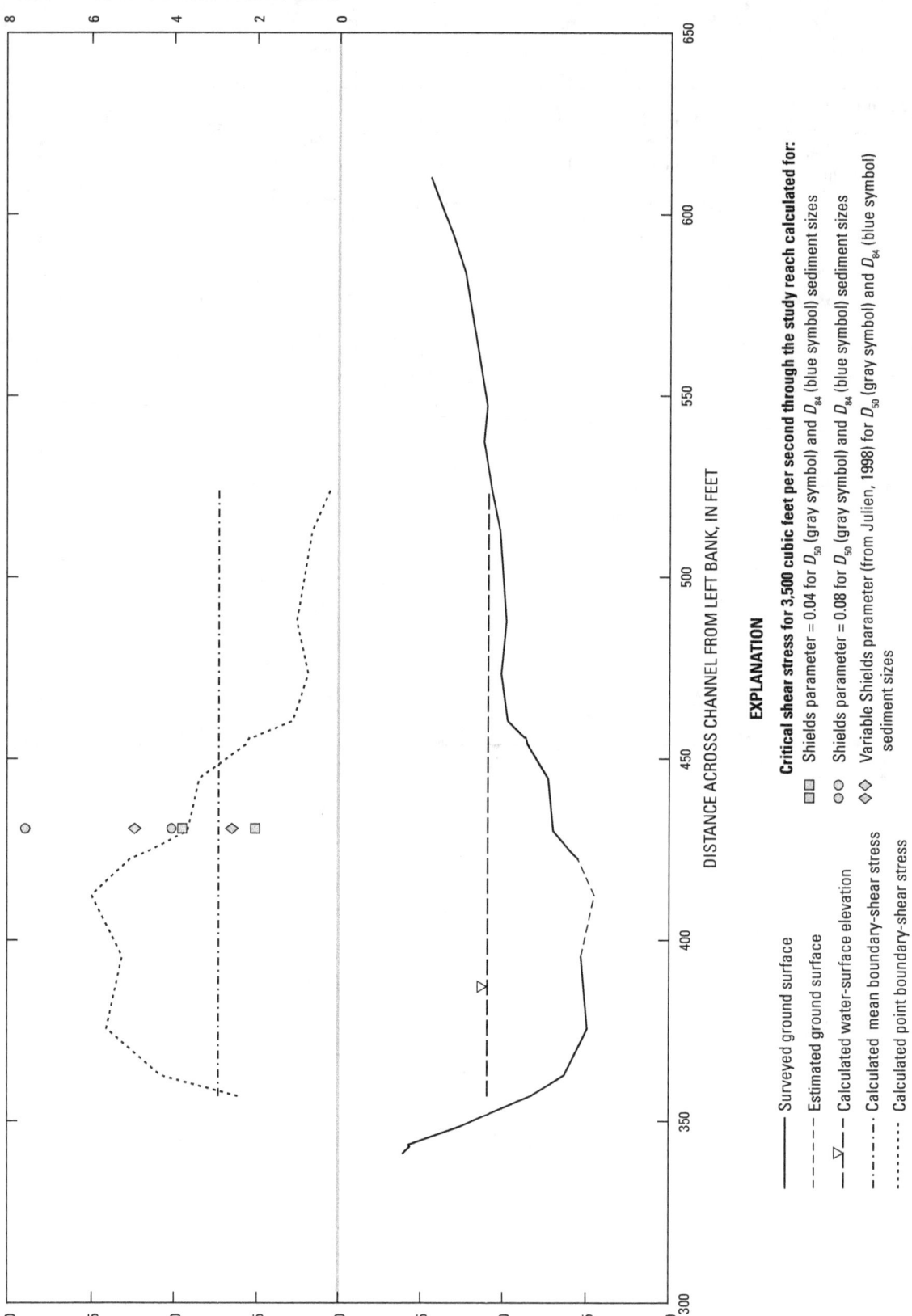

Figure 15. Calculated mean and point boundary-shear stresses at cross section 400 and calculated critical shear stresses for movement of selected sediment sizes between cross sections 500 and 400, Madison River downstream from Earthquake Lake, Montana.

Cross Sections 1400–1300, Earthquake Lake Outlet

At the upstream end of the spillway, between cross sections 1400 and 1300, the right part of the bed was sampled using the pebble-count method (table 4, fig. 14). Through this subreach, the mean boundary-shear stresses are difficult to compare to the critical shear stresses because the mean boundary-shear stresses increased by about 500 percent between cross sections 1400 and 1300 (fig. 16). For the purposes of this discussion, it is assumed that the bed sample is representative of the bed material at a midpoint between cross sections 1400 and 1300, and that the mean-boundary shear stress varies linearly between the two cross sections. The critical shear stresses for the D_{50} particle size calculated using all of the Shields parameters are smaller than the mean boundary-shear stress for the 3,500-ft^3/s threshold streamflow (fig. 16A, inset), indicating that most of the D_{50} particles along the right side of the bed could move at the 3,500-ft^3/s threshold streamflow.

The critical shear stresses for the D_{84} particle size calculated using the Shields parameter of 0.04 is smaller than the mean boundary-shear stress calculated for the 3,500-ft^3/s threshold streamflow, indicating that some of these larger materials along the right side of the bed could move at the 3,500-ft^3/s threshold streamflow. However, critical shear stresses for the D_{84} particle size calculated using the variable Shields parameter and the Shields parameter of 0.08 are both larger than the mean boundary-shear stress calculated for the 3,500-ft^3/s threshold streamflow, indicating that most of these larger size fractions along the right part of the bed near the outlet are not likely to move at the 3,500-ft^3/s threshold streamflow.

In summary, most of the D_{50} particle sizes along the right side of the bed between cross sections 1400 and 1300 could be moved by the 3,500-ft^3/s threshold streamflow (assuming the bed sample is representative of the bed material at a midpoint between cross sections 1400 and 1300, and that the mean-boundary shear stress varies linearly between cross sections 1400 and 1300 as depicted in figure 16A). However, most of the D_{84} particle sizes probably would not move.

Limitations of the Estimates for Potential for Bed-Material Movement

Assumptions for using HEC-RAS to calculate hydraulic variables such as water-surface elevation, hydraulic radius, streamflow depth, and mean boundary-shear stress (U.S. Army Corps of Engineers, 2008b, p. 2–20) include:

1. Steady flow–streamflow does not change with time;

2. Gradually varied flow–depths do not abruptly change along the channel;

3. One-dimensional flow–magnitude and direction of the velocity vectors at a cross section are equal—the flow at a cross section is all moving in one direction down the channel, with no cross-currents or diversions; and

4. Thalweg slopes that are less than about 0.10 ft/ft.

Point boundary-shear stresses calculated as a function of streamflow depth and energy slope also are affected by these assumptions. In addition to the assumptions for using HEC-RAS to calculate hydraulic variables, use of equation 3 is based on the assumption that the channel cross section has a regular or trapezoidal shape that is at least 10 times wider than it is deep (Elliott, 2002).

Few natural streams completely satisfy these assumptions including the Madison River in the study area. Flow at many locations along the study reach, especially near cross section 700, varies rapidly because large boulders disrupt the flow and cross-section shapes (and consequently streamflow depths) change substantially from place to place along the channel.

The Shields parameter used for calculating critical shear stress (equation 4) can vary according to energy slope and bed-material characteristics such as the sediment-size distribution, shape, orientation, and how tightly particles are packed together. As discussed in the section "Critical Shear Stress," investigators have used Shields parameter values ranging from 0.01 to 0.11. Large Shields parameters have been used to calculate critical shear stresses for high-gradient streams, such as the Madison River (Mueller and others, 2005). Therefore, bed material in the Madison River might be associated with critical shear stress values at or above the upper ranges of critical shear stresses presented in this report. In addition, larger, more erosion-resistant materials likely exist in the parts of the channel where high-flow depths and velocities prevented sediment sampling. Movement of these materials might require higher mean boundary-shear stresses and flow rates than estimated in this report. Characterization of sediment sizes in the center of the stream and observation of bed-material movement for a range of streamflows could provide information to help refine the Shields parameter and critical-shear stress estimates for bed materials in the Madison River downstream from Earthquake Lake.

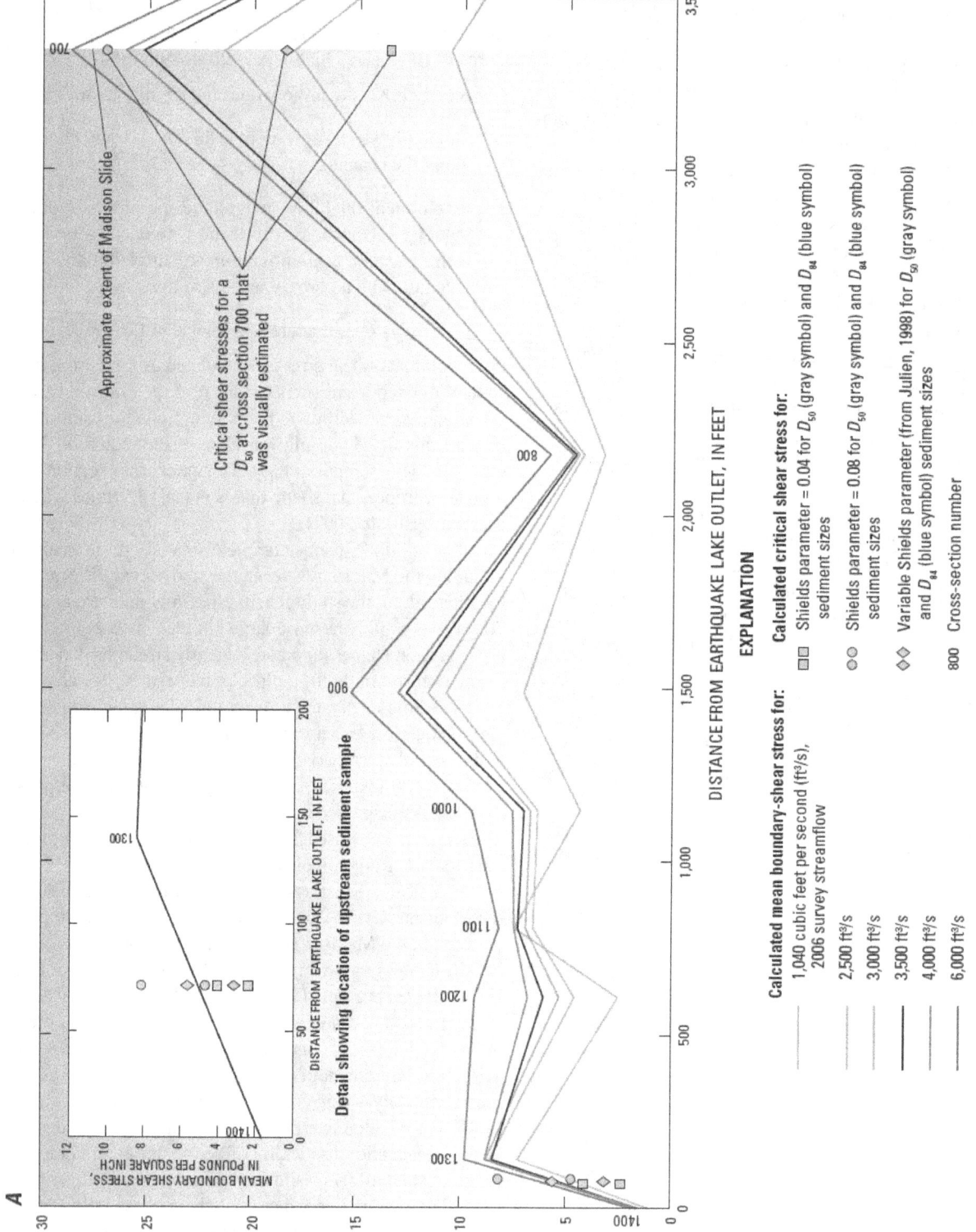

Figure 16. Calculated mean boundary-shear stress at various streamflows and calculated critical shear stresses for selected sediment sizes, Madison River downstream from Earthquake Lake, Montana. *A*, From cross section 1400 to cross section 700. *B*, From cross section 700 to cross section 400.

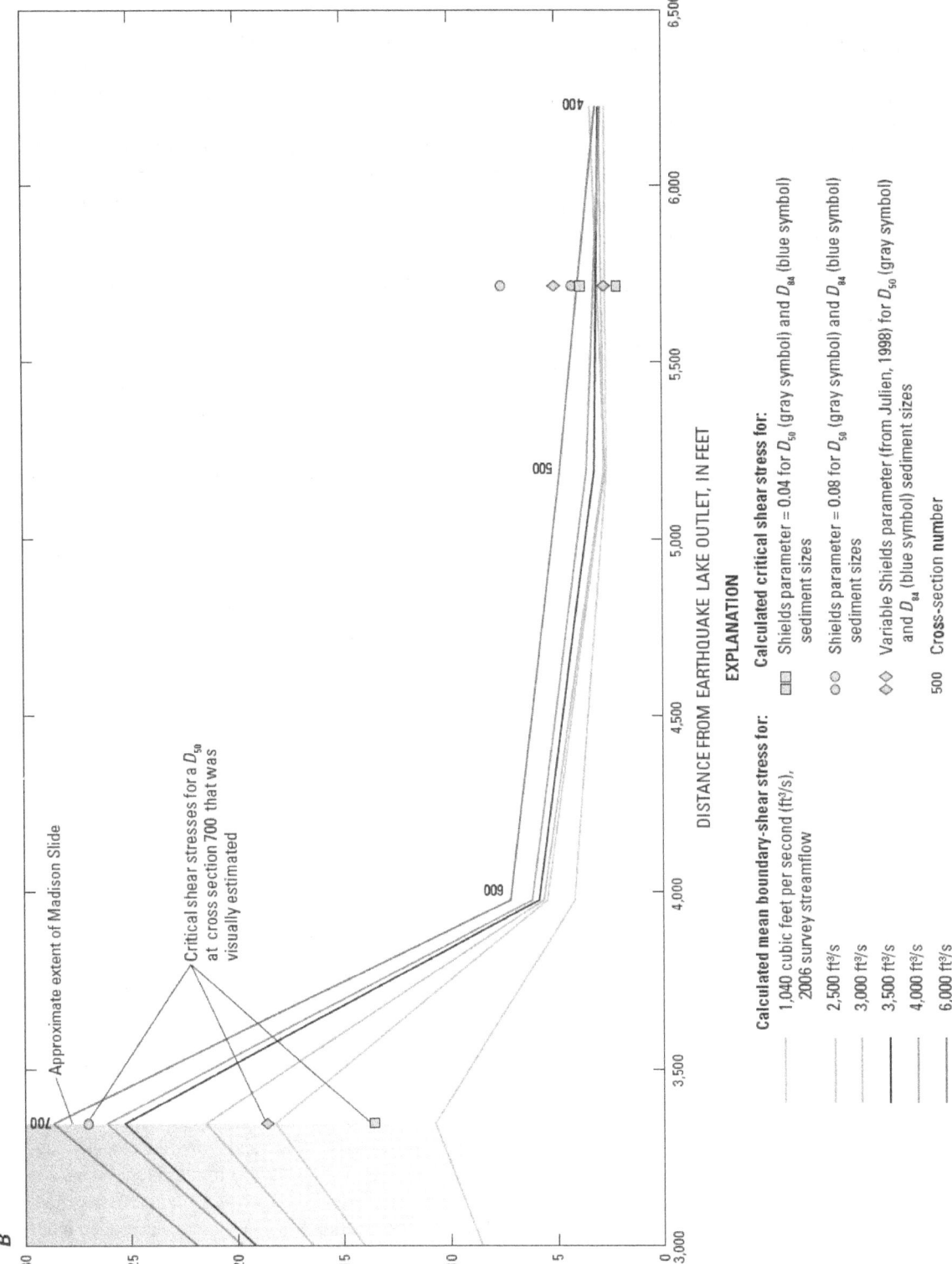

Figure 16. Calculated mean boundary-shear stress at various streamflows and calculated critical shear stresses for selected sediment sizes, Madison River downstream from Earthquake Lake, Montana. *A*, From cross section 1400 to cross section 700. *B*, From cross section 700 to cross section 400.—Continued

Summary and Conclusions

The 1959 Hebgen Lake earthquake caused a massive landslide (Madison Slide) that dammed the Madison River and formed Earthquake Lake. The U.S. Army Corps of Engineers excavated a spillway through the Madison Slide to permit outflow from Earthquake Lake. In June 1970, high streamflows in the Madison River severely eroded the spillway and damaged the roadway embankment along U.S. Highway 287 north of the channel. Flooding in 1971 and 1986 caused additional erosion of the spillway channel and roadway embankment. Investigations undertaken following the 1970 and 1971 flood events concluded that substantial erosion through and downstream from the spillway could be expected for streamflows greater than 3,500 cubic feet per second (ft^3/s). Accordingly, PPL-Montana, the current (2011) owner of Hebgen Dam upstream from Earthquake Lake, has tried to manage releases from Hebgen Lake to prevent streamflows [as measured at U.S. Geological Survey (USGS) gaging station 06038800] from exceeding 3,500 cubic feet per second (ft^3/s).

Management of flow releases from Hebgen Lake to prevent streamflows at USGS gaging station 06038800 from exceeding the 3,500-ft^3/s threshold streamflow is difficult. Flooding of Cabin Creek and Beaver Creek, which enter the Madison River between Hebgen Lake and the Earthquake Lake outlet, can cause streamflows at the outlet and at gaging station 06038800 to exceed the 3,500-ft^3/s threshold streamflow even when streamflow releases from Hebgen Lake are minimal.

The 3,500-ft^3/s threshold streamflow has been questioned for two main reasons. First, no road damage was reported downstream from the Earthquake Lake outlet in 1993, 1996, and 1997 when streamflows exceeded the 3,500-ft^3/s threshold streamflow. This lack of road damage during relatively high streamflows might indicate that the channel has become armored and is no longer as susceptible to erosion as it was in the 1970s and 1980s. Second, the 3,500-ft^3/s threshold streamflow generally precludes releases of higher flows that could be beneficial to the blue-ribbon trout fishery downstream in the Madison River.

In response to concerns about minimizing streamflow downstream from Earthquake Lake and the possible armoring of the spillway, the USGS, in cooperation with the Madison River Fisheries Technical Advisory Committee (MADTAC; Bureau of Land Management; Montana Department of Environmental Quality; Montana Fish, Wildlife and Parks; PPL-Montana; U.S. Department of Agriculture Forest Service – Gallatin National Forest; and U.S. Fish and Wildlife Service), conducted a study to determine movement of the Madison River channel downstream from Earthquake Lake and to investigate the potential for bed material movement along the same reach. The purpose of this report is to present information about the lateral and vertical movement of the Madison River from 1970 to 2006 for a 1-mile reach downstream from Earthquake Lake and for Raynolds Pass Bridge, and to provide an analysis of the potential for bed-material movement so that

MADTAC can evaluate the applicability of the 3,500-ft^3/s threshold streamflow for initiation of damaging erosion.

Channel cross sections originally surveyed by the USGS in 1971 were resurveyed in 2006. Incremental channel-movement distances were determined by comparing the stream centerlines from 14 aerial photographs taken between 1970 and 2006. Depths of channel incision and aggregation were determined by comparing the 2006 and 1971 cross-section and water-surface data. Particle sizes of bed and bank materials were measured in 2006 and 2008 using the pebble-count method and sieve analyses. A one-dimensional hydraulic-flow model (HEC-RAS) was used to calculate mean boundary-shear stresses for various streamflows; these calculated boundary-shear stresses were compared to calculated critical-shear stresses for the bed materials to determine the potential for bed-material movement.

The Madison River channel through the Madison slide downstream from Earthquake Lake (the spillway) has steep longitudinal slopes [up to 0.046 feet per feet (ft/ft)] and, therefore, can transport large quantities of materials from the bed and banks. Because Earthquake Lake tends to trap sediment, the spillway is prone to incision and lateral movement. Additionally, the channel banks along the spillway are extremely high and the bank slopes are almost equal to the angle of repose for the bank material. As the river undercuts the banks, large amounts of material are deposited into the channel, further contributing to channel instability. In contrast, the longitudinal slopes downstream from the spillway are not as steep. Consequently, much of the material removed from the spillway can be deposited downstream, which can lead to channel aggradation, widening, and braiding downstream from the Madison Slide.

Between 1971 and 2006, the Madison River channel has moved laterally to varying degrees throughout the study area. A comparison of lateral channel movement distances to annual peak streamflows shows that streamflows higher than 3,500 ft^3/s generally were followed by lateral channel movement except from 1991 to 1992 and possibly from 1996 to 1997. Where more than one year lapsed between aerial photographs, it is not possible to discern whether the channel moved gradually or all in one year. It also is unclear whether the channel moved in response to one peak flow, to several peak flows, or to sustained flows. The channel moved between 2002 and 2005 even though streamflows during that period were less than the 3,500-ft^3/s threshold streamflow.

The channel has incised to varying degrees through the Madison Slide. Between 1971 and 2006, the channel bed incised by as much as 5 feet (ft) at the Earthquake Lake outlet (cross section 1400) and as much as 12 ft at cross section 1000. Near cross section 800, the stream has eroded into fill that was mechanically placed between 1970 and 1975 along the steep right bank between the stream and the road.

The channel appears to have changed the least at the downstream end of the Madison Slide, along a subreach from near cross section 800 to cross section 700. The stream in this subreach could be composed of erosion-resistant materials similar to the large dolomite boulder on the right bank that was deposited by the Madison Slide and the dolomite outcrop on the left bank.

Channel movement also was noted downstream from the Madison Slide. The channel has aggraded, moved laterally, and incised a new lower channel between cross sections 600 and 500. The channel has moved laterally and aggraded at cross section 400.

Near Raynolds Pass Bridge, about 3 mile (mi) downstream from Earthquake Lake, elevations across the channel have changed by -1.4 ft to +1.9 ft, but these changes were local in nature and could represent a few rocks or depressions in the bed. The right bank at cross section 300 was about 5 ft lower in the 2006 survey than the 1971 survey; this difference could indicate erosion at the right back or could be due to the two surveys being in slightly different locations. Overall, it does not appear that the materials eroded from the Madison Slide are causing aggradation near the Raynolds Pass Bridge.

Maximum lateral-movement distances of the channel between 1970 and 2006 (the maximum distances between the centerlines from all of the aerial photographs) were 150 ft near the upstream end of the spillway near cross section 1100, 370 ft downstream from the spillway between cross sections 400 and 500, and 560 ft about 1 mile downstream from the Madison Slide. All channel movement-distances are plus or minus (+/-) 30 ft due to potential errors in rectifying the aerial photographs.

Channel movement was determined from aerial photographs and sparse survey data. A relation between streamflow and channel movement is difficult to determine because more than a year passed between most of the aerial photographs and more than 30 years passed between the most recent surveys. Resurveying cross sections and water-surface elevations more frequently (either annually or after high streamflows) could better define the relation between streamflow and lateral and vertical channel movement.

The ability of a river to move particles on the bed is a function of the boundary shear stress or the force per unit area that a river exerts on its bed in the direction of flow. The critical shear stress is the shear stress required to initiate movement of sediment of a specific size from the bed. If the boundary shear stress is larger than the critical shear stress for a given streamflow, the bed material is likely to move, potentially resulting in channel adjustments. Critical shear stresses were calculated for the D_{50}, D_{65}, and D_{84} sediment sizes at two locations: near the upstream end of the Madison Slide and downstream from the Madison Slide.

Some of the critical shear stresses calculated for the D_{50} particle sizes along the right side of the bed between cross sections 500 and 400, and all of the critical shear stresses calculated for the D_{50} particle sizes along the right side of the bed between cross sections 1400 and 1300 are less than the mean boundary-shear stress generated by the 3,500-ft^3/s threshold streamflow. These comparisons indicate that these median particle sizes could move at the 3,500-ft^3/s threshold streamflow. In contrast, all of the critical shear stresses calculated for

the D_{84} particle sizes along the right side of the bed at between cross sections 500 and 400 and most of the critical shear stresses calculated for the D_{84} particle sizes along the right side of the bed between cross sections 1400 and 1300 are greater than the mean boundary-shear stress generated by a streamflow of 3,500 ft^3/s. These comparisons indicate that most of these larger particles probably will not move at the 3,500-ft^3/s threshold streamflow. This lack of movement for the larger particles at the 3,500-ft^3/s threshold streamflow could lead to further armoring of the bed as the D_{50} and smaller-sized particles are removed from the bed and transported downstream. However, these smaller particles could be replenished by particles eroded from the steep spillway banks.

The Shields parameter values from 0.04 to 0.08 that were used to calculate critical shear stresses could be conservative for a high-gradient stream such as the Madison River. A higher, less conservative, Shields parameter would result in higher critical-shear stresses, meaning that higher streamflows would be required to move material than those reported herein. In addition, larger, more erosion-resistant materials likely exist in the parts of the channel where high-flow depths and velocities prevented sediment sampling. Movement of these materials might require higher mean boundary-shear stresses and flow rates than estimated in this report. Characterization of sediment sizes in the center of the stream and observation of bed-material movement for a range of streamflows could provide information to help refine the Shields parameter and critical-shear stress estimates for bed materials in the Madison River downstream from Earthquake Lake.

References Cited

Dingman, S.L., 2009, Fluvial Hydraulics: New York, Oxford University Press, 559 p.

Elliott, J.G., and Hammack, L.A., 2000, Entrainment of riparian gravel and cobbles in an alluvial reach of a regulated river: Regulated Rivers–Research and Management, v. 16, no. 1, p. 37–50. (Also available at *http://dx.doi.org*/10.1002/(SICI)1099-1646(200001/02)16:1<37::AID-RRR564>3.0.CO;2-V.)

Elliott, J.G., 2002, Bed-material entrainment potential, Roaring Fork River at Basalt, Colorado: U.S. Geological Survey Water-Resources Investigations Report 02–4223, 33 p.

Foundation and Materials Consultants, Inc., 1972, Report on preliminary foundation investigation, Quake Lake Dam, Madison County, Montana: Missoula, Mont., Foundation and Materials Consultants, Inc. [prepared for U.S. Department of Agriculture Forest Service–Northern Region, Missoula, Mont., variously paged].

Hadley, J.B., 1964, Landslides and related phenomena accompanying the Hebgen Lake Earthquake of August 17, 1959: U.S. Geological Survey Professional Paper 435-K, 31 p.

Heitmuller, F.T., and Asquith, W.H., 2008, Potential for bed-material entrainment in selected streams of the Edwards Plateau—Edwards, Kimble, and Real Counties, Texas, and vicinity: U.S. Geological Survey Scientific Investigations Report 2008–5017, 76 p.

Henderson, F.M., 1966, Open channel flow: New York, MacMillan, 522 p.

Hughes, M.L., McDowell, W.A., and Marcus, W.A., 2006, Accuracy assessment of georectified aerial photographs–Implications for measuring lateral channel movement in a GIS: Geomorphology, v. 74, p. 1–16. (Also available at *http://dx.doi.org/10.1016/j.geomorph.2005.07.001.*)

Johnson, M.V., and Omang, R.J., 1972, Degradation of the Earthquake Lake outflow channel, southwestern Montana: U.S. Geological Survey Professional Paper 800-C, 4 p.

Julien, P.Y., 1998, Erosion and sedimentation: Cambridge, United Kingdom, Cambridge University Press, 280 p.

Montana Fish, Wildlife and Parks, 2010, Metadata for Montana Blue and Red Ribbon Streams, accessed January 30, 2010, at *http://fwp.mt.gov/doingBusiness/reference/gisData/metadata/blueredstreams.htm.*

Montana State Library, 2007, Metadata for Montana 2005 color NAIP orthophotos, 12-kilometer tiles: Montana Natural Resources Information System, accessed January 29, 2007, at *http://gisportal.msl.mt.gov/GPT9/catalog/search/viewMetadataDetails.page?uuid={539F25E9-36E3-4F94-A174-FF609D8192CC}.*

Mueller, E.R., Nelson, J.M., and Pitlick, John, 2005, Variation in the reference Shields stress for bed load transport in gravel-bed streams and rivers: Water Resources Research, v. 41, W04006, 10 p. (Also available at *http://dx.doi.org/10.1029/2004WR003692.*)

Parrett, C.P., and Johnson, D.R, 2004, Methods for estimating flood frequency in Montana based on data through water year 1998: U.S. Geological Survey Water-Resources Investigations Report 03–4308, 101 p.

Shields, A.F., 1936, Application of similarity principles and turbulence research to bedload movement: *translated from* Anwendung der Aehnlichkeitsmechanik und der Turbulenzforschung auf die Geschiebewegung: Mitteilung Preussischen Versuchanstalt für Wasserbau und Schiffbau, Berlin, No. 26, *by* Ott, W.P., and van Uchelen, J.C., California Institute of Technology, Hydrodynamics Laboratory, Publication number 176, Pasadena, Calif., 167, 43 p.

U.S. Army Corps of Engineers, 1972, Report on Quake Lake Project, Madison River, Montana: Omaha, Nebr., U.S. Army Corps of Engineers [variously paged].

U.S. Army Corps of Engineers, Hydrologic Engineering Center, 2008a, HEC-RAS, River analysis system user's manual, version 4.0: Hydrologic Engineering Center, Davis, Calif., 733 p.

U.S. Army Corps of Engineers, Hydrologic Engineering Center, 2008b, HEC-RAS, River analysis system hydraulic reference manual, version 4.0: Davis, Calif., 411 p.

U.S. Army Corps of Engineers, Hydrologic Engineering Center, 2008c, HEC-RAS, River analysis system applications guide, version 4.0:, Davis, Calif., 351 p.

U.S. Geological Survey, 2007a, National Aerial Photography Program (NAPP), [U.S. Geological Survey Center for Earth Resources Observation & Science (EROS)], accessed January 1, 2007, at *http://eros.usgs.gov/#/Find_Data/Products_and_Data_Available/NAPP.*

U.S. Geological Survey, 2007b, National High Altitude Photography (NHAP), [U.S. Geological Survey Center for Earth Resources Observation & Science (EROS)], accessed January 1, 2007, at *http://eros.usgs.gov/#/Find_Data/Products_and_Data_Available/NHAP.*

U.S. Geological Survey, 2008, Peak streamflow for Montana, accessed June 11, 2008, at *http://nwis.waterdata.usgs.gov/mt/nwis/peak.*

U.S. Geological Survey, 2009, U.S. Geological Survey Photographic Library, accessed February 12, 2009, at *http://libraryphoto.cr.usgs.gov/cgi-bin/search.cgi?search_mode=noPunct&free_form=Madison&free_form=Slide&free_form=dolomite&free_form=.*

Wilcock, P.R., and McArdell, B.W., 1993, Surface-based fractional transport rates–Mobilization thresholds and partial transport of a sand-gravel sediment: Water Resources Research v. 29, no. 4, p. 1297–1312. (Also available at *http://dx.doi.org/10.1029/92WR02748.*)

Wolman, M.G., 1954, A method of sampling coarse river-bed material: American Geophysical Union Transactions, v. 35, p. 951–956.

Appendix 1. Aerial Photographs and Locations of Stream Centerlines and Cross Sections of the Madison River Downstream from Earthquake Lake, Montana.

Incremental-channel movement was determined from 14 aerial photographs taken between 1970 and 2006. Aerial photographs from the years 1980, 1981, 1987, 1990, and 2002 are not included in this appendix because substantial channel movement was not observed from those photographs, except for the 40 ft (plus or minus 30 ft) of movement at cross section 700 and movement towards the road about 0.25 mi downstream from cross section 400, both observed in the 1987 photograph. The 2006 digital orthophotograph was used as a reference to which the earlier photographs were rectified. On each aerial photograph, two stream centerlines were drawn: one centerline corresponded to the stream location shown on the photograph, and the other centerline corresponded to the stream location from the previous aerial photograph. In the more braided subreaches downstream from the Madison Slide, centerlines were drawn along the dominant flow-conveying channel at the date and streamflow corresponding to the aerial photograph. At higher streamflows, more than one of the braided channels could be inundated, and the differences between the centerlines would not be as dramatic. As discussed in the section "Methods," channel-movement distances measured between centerlines on the aerial photographs are plus or minus 30 ft, due to potential errors in rectification of the photographs.

The nine aerial photographs (figs. A–1 to A–9) are located in the CD–ROM on the inside back cover of this report. This appendix also can be downloaded from *http://pubs.usgs.gov/sir/2012/5024/.*

Publishing support provided by the:
    Denver and Rolla Publishing Service Centers

For more information concerning this publication, contact:
    Director, Montana Water Science Center
    U.S. Geological Survey
    3162 Bozeman Ave.
    Helena, MT 59601
    (406) 457–5900

Or visit the Montana Water Science Center Web site at:
    http://mt.water.usgs.gov/

USGS

Chase and McCarthy— Lateral and Vertical Channel Movement and Potential for Bed-Material Movement on the Madison River, Montana—SIR 2012–5024

ISBN 978-1-4113-3363-5